STRIVING FOR EXCELLENCE:
ANCIENT GREEK CHILDHOOD
AND THE OLYMPIC SPIRIT

*A special supplement to the exhibition organized
by the Hood Museum of Art, Dartmouth College*

COMING OF AGE IN ANCIENT GREECE:
IMAGES OF CHILDHOOD
FROM THE CLASSICAL PAST

STRIVING FOR EXCELLENCE: ANCIENT GREEK CHILDHOOD AND THE OLYMPIC SPIRIT

Jenifer Neils and John H. Oakley

With a contribution by
Christine Kondoleon

With the assistance of
Katherine Hart

A special supplement to the exhibition organized by
the Hood Museum of Art, Dartmouth College

COMING OF AGE IN ANCIENT GREECE: IMAGES OF CHILDHOOD FROM THE CLASSICAL PAST

ALEXANDER S. ONASSIS PUBLIC BENEFIT FOUNDATION (USA)

Published by the Alexander S. Onassis Public Benefit Foundation (USA)

© 2004 by the Alexander S. Onassis Public Benefit Foundation (USA), New York, N.Y. 10022

ONASSIS CULTURAL CENTER, 645 Fifth Avenue, New York, N.Y. 10022
January 22–April 15, 2004

CONTRIBUTORS TO THE EXHIBITION
The exhibition was organized by the Hood Museum of Art, Dartmouth College, and curated by
Jenifer Neils, Ruth Coulter Heede Professor, Department of Art History and Art, Case Western Reserve
University, Cleveland, Ohio, and John H. Oakley, Chairman, Department of Classical Studies, Chancellor
Professor, and Forrest D. Murden, Jr., Professor, The College of William and Mary, Williamsburg, Virginia.
The exhibition "Coming of Age in Ancient Greece" has been made possible in part by the National Endowment
for the Humanities, promoting excellence in the humanities. The Alexander S. Onassis Public Benefit
Foundation (USA) is also a major supporter of the exhibition.

Design
Daniel B. Kershaw

Graphics
Sophia Geronimus

Lighting
Anita Jorgensen

Installation
David Latouche

Conservator
Leslie Gat

CONTRIBUTORS TO THE CATALOGUE
Authors
Jenifer Neils
John H. Oakley

Contributing Author
Christine Kondoleon

Editor
Pamela Barr

Design
Sophia Geronimus

Printing
Random Printing, Inc.

This catalogue was produced for "Striving for Excellence: Ancient Greek Childhood and the Olympic Spirit,"
a special supplement to the exhibition organized by the Hood Museum of Art, Dartmouth College,
"Coming of Age in Ancient Greece: Images of Childhood from the Classical Past."

FRONT COVER: cat. D. *Kylix with Pentathletes* (detail). Attic red-figure *kylix*, attributed to Onesimos, ca. 500–490 B.C.
Museum of Fine Arts, Boston, Henry Lillie Pierce Fund, 1901 (01.8020)

BACK COVER: cat. A. *Bell-shaped Doll or Idol.* Boeotian terracotta, Late Geometric, ca. 720–700 B.C.
Museum of Fine Arts, Boston, Henry Lillie Pierce Fund, 1898 (98.891)

CONTENTS

FOREWORD

The Onassis Foundation (USA) proudly presents at the Onassis Cultural Center in New York City the exhibition "Coming of Age in Ancient Greece: Images of Childhood from the Classical Past" curated admirably by Dr. Jenifer Neils and Dr. John H. Oakley and organized by the Hood Museum of Art, Dartmouth College, in the most thorough and scientific way.

After a first most successful presentation at the Hood Museum of Art and before moving to the Cincinnati Art Museum and the J. Paul Getty Museum, this important exhibition will offer to the public of New York a rare and exciting view of coming of age in antiquity.

By focusing on the rather unexamined theme of childhood in ancient Greece, we understand better how those children grew up to become magnificent artists, outstanding statesmen, great philosophers, and model citizens who lighted a torch that has enlightened the world over the centuries.

The exhibition at the Onassis Cultural Center will offer a special section, in addition to the exhibition, "Striving for Excellence: Ancient Greek Childhood and the Olympic Spirit" with masterpieces from the Boston Museum of Fine Arts and the Hood Museum of Art.

If indeed the future of humanity is in the hands of our children, it is perhaps high time to delve more deeply and understand better how a glorious past, when children in ancient Greece were instilled with love for noble emulation and excellence, has defined our present and can improve our future.

Stelio Papadimitriou
President
Alexander S. Onassis Public Benefit Foundation

PREFACE

This book commemorates the first major art exhibition devoted to the subject of childhood in ancient Greece. Organized by the Hood Museum of Art at Dartmouth College, with crucial support from both the National Endowment for the Humanities and the Alexander S. Onassis Public Benefit Foundation, this exhibition will be seen by over 100,000 people throughout the United States before it closes. Most fittingly, its presentation at the Onassis Cultural Center in New York early in 2004 falls within the same year that the Olympic Games return to the country where they were founded in 776 B.C. This joyful occasion also marks the first time that the modern Olympics have been held in Greece since their beginnings in Athens 108 years ago.

The education and training of ancient children and adolescents in the subjects of letters, music, and athletics is one of the major themes of "Coming of Age in Ancient Greece." In the Onassis Foundation's presentation of the exhibition, the curators have also drawn special attention to the important part played by games and physical contests in nurturing the body as well as the mind.

The integration of the intellectual with the physical continues to this day in the educational philosophy of institutions of higher education in this country. Dartmouth College has always promoted the essential role that athletics play in the development of the individual. Indeed, each year the College symbolically awards the Hood Museum of Art's Panathenaic amphora by the Berlin Painter (cat. H) to one of our undergraduates who has "in the course of the year made a significant and distinctive contribution in his life or his work to the life of the college." The amphora was originally given as a prize to an athlete who participated in quadrennial games that were held in ancient Greece to honor the goddess Athena. At Dartmouth, the individuals who have been awarded the honor have their names inscribed on a plaque adjacent to the amphora in the museum.

On behalf of my colleagues at Dartmouth College and the Hood Museum of Art, I extend congratulations to the Alexander S. Onassis Public Benefit Foundation (USA) on the successful opening of "Coming of Age in Ancient Greece" at their New York Cultural Center. I seize this opportunity, as well, to extend best wishes to Greece and to the Greek people on the return of the Olympic Games to the country of their origin.

James Wright
President
Dartmouth College

INTRODUCTION

Childhood is said to be a universal experience. Certainly the fulfillment of children's common needs—for nurturing, stability, guidance, affection, education, and play—affects the quality of the life that they will lead as an adult. What children in all cultures learn through their interaction with others provides a model for behavior. We also now know that children themselves influence aspects of their lives, in matters as simple as responding to some toys more than others or as complex as the effect of their varying relationships with members of their household. Children's lives with family, other household members, and peers also shape how they treat others as well as the next generation of children. The study of society's images of children as well as of texts pertaining to rearing practices and parental attitudes toward their offspring is integral to understanding a culture as a whole.

The experiences of individual children are far from universal, both in earlier ages and in our own. Their inherited traits, dispositions, and talents differ. Economics and status usually govern a child's potential as a future member of society. In the case of ancient Athens, it was gender and access to education that cultivated the thinker and the philosopher and the fact of citizenship that created opportunity for economic prosperity. Our information about the experience of individual children in ancient cultures is limited, however. We know, instead, of writings that prescribe how children should be educated or their characters guided and formed under their parents' or teachers' tutelage. And while we cannot recover their voices, even through adults writing in retrospect about their own upbringings, we can collect images of young lives and interpret—through comparative analysis with other visual evidence and by piecing together historical information and fragmentary textual references—what they may have meant to their original audience. This is the first major exhibition to bring art and artifacts on childhood in ancient Greece together for study and, as such, is just the beginning of a long process of discovery.

Without question, one of the greatest influences on Western ideals, government, and education has been that of ancient Greece. Thus, when presenting and shaping an exhibition about images of childhood made in a culture more than two thousand years ago—and one that has had a profound effect on the art of Western societies in Europe and the United States—the curators of "Coming of Age in Ancient Greece," Jenifer Neils and John H. Oakley, felt it important to present images of both the children of citizens, which are those that predominate, and of children who, while part of the household, held the status of slaves or servants. Thus, while some objects in this exhibition express ancient Greeks' ideals of behavior, their interest in dramatic narrative, and even their sense of humor, they also sometimes reflect practices that mainstream modern Western culture has, over time, rejected. Underlying these images are echoes of the complex human interactions of the men, women, and children who lived in an evolving social and political system subjected to the stresses of war, disease, and survival.

Equally important to the curators was to examine the visual record of boys in relation to that of girls. Girls in ancient Greece, especially those who were the daughters of citizens, had a much narrower world than boys. However, there are areas of similarity, such as games that they played or their early years as infants. In this catalogue, the curators have presented the material through two thematic sections—one for each gender—that follow the differing activities for male and female. For the Onassis Cultural Center's presentation of the exhibition, Drs. Neils and Oakley have also created a section that reveals the stress placed on athletics in the formation of a male youth's character and development of physical prowess. The Alexander S. Onassis Public Benefit Foundation, the curators, and the Hood Museum of Art are particularly indebted to the Museum of Fine Arts, Boston, and to Dr. Christine Kondoleon, George D. and Margo Behrakis Curator of Greek and Roman Art, for their loan of a number of spectacular objects related to athletic contests in ancient Greece.

It is the generosity of all lenders to exhibitions such as this that makes the existence of such an ambitious exhibition possible and to them we extend our deepest gratitude. The support of the National Endowment for the Humanities and the Alexander S. Onassis Public Benefit Foundation (USA) has also been of crucial importance to "Coming of Age in Ancient Greece: Images of Childhood from the Classical Past." On behalf of the curators and the Hood Museum of Art, I would like to express our profound appreciation and gratitude to the honorable President of the Onassis Foundation, Stelio Papadimitriou, and to the board of the Foundation and its representatives in the United States, the Executive Director, Ambassador Loucas Tsilas, and the Director of Cultural Events, Amalia Cosmetatou. Without their vision and enthusiasm, this exhibition would not have been possible.

Katherine Hart
Barbara C. & Harvey P. Hood 1918 Curator of Academic Programming, Hood Museum of Art, Dartmouth College

Timarete, the daughter of Timaretos, before her wedding,
has dedicated her tambourine, her pretty ball, the net
that shielded her hair, her hair, and her girls' dresses
to Artemis of the Lake, a girl to a girl, as is fit.
You, daughter of Leto, hold your hand over the child
Timarete, and protect the pure girl in a pure way.

—*Anthologia Palatina* 6.280

Fig. 1 (COA cat. 124). *Gravestone of the Girl Melisto.* Attic marble grave
stele, ca. 340 B.C. Harvard University Art Museums, Arthur M. Sackler
Museum, Cambridge, Alpheus Hyatt Purchasing and Gifts for Special
Uses Funds in memory of Katherine Brewster Taylor, as tribute to her
many years at the Fogg Museum

A GIRL'S LIFE IN ANCIENT GREECE

John H. Oakley

Greek art tells us much about a girl's childhood in ancient Greece. Not only does it illustrate various phases and aspects of it, but Greek art also gives us insight into the way adults viewed their children while supplying details about childhood not provided by other sources. Naturally, the specific nature of a girl's upbringing varied depending upon several factors, including her social class, where she lived in the Greek world, and when. While the artistic, archaeological, and literary sources do provide us with a good general sense of what a girl's childhood was like, many specific aspects about it remain unknown. We know the most about childhood in Classical Athens (fifth and fourth centuries B.C.), and much of the picture presented here will focus on the artistic evidence from that city during this period.

Birth

Mortal human birth was a rare subject in ancient Greek art. Probably the best-known representation of birth is a Cypriot terracotta group from the sixth century B.C.[1] The three figures comprising the group consist of the mother seated upon the lap of a kneeling assistant who has her arms wrapped around the mother's waist and a second female helper who sits and bends over ready to take the child from between the mother's legs when it is born. In Classical art, birth is normally not represented; rather occasionally, the labor leading up to it can be inferred by the way the mother is depicted. A small group of Athenian marble gravestones from the second half of the fourth century is the most well-known example (COA, cat. 19).

Although depictions of mortal births are rare, those of the gods and heroes are much more common. Their births, however, are usually not normal but fantastic. By far the most popular birth scene in Greek art is Athena's. She was born from Zeus' head after he swallowed her mother, Metis, because it had been foretold that her child would be more powerful than its father. A well-preserved version of this scene decorates an Attic black-figure amphora from Group E (Fig. 2, COA cat. 5). As is normally the case, a small Athena, fully armed, emerges from the head of a seated Zeus who is surrounded by other deities present to witness the birth. Before him stand two Eileithyiai, birth goddesses, who raise their right hands toward his head in order to soothe the pain of birth. Behind them stands Ares, the god of war, the male counterpart to

Fig. 2 (COA cat. 5). *Birth of Athena*. Attic black-figure amphora, attributed to Group E, ca. 550 B.C. Yale University Art Gallery, New Haven, Leonard C. Hanna, Jr., B.A. 1913 Fund (1983.22)

Athena the warrior—a particularly appropriate divinity to be present. Apollo playing his kithara and Dionysos both stand behind Zeus and fill out the picture. Athena was the patron goddess of Athens. Thus, it is not surprising that this scene was particularly popular on Athenian vases and that it was depicted in the east pediment of the Parthenon, the goddess's main temple on the Acropolis. The goddess Aphrodite, like Athena, was born fully grown, as if she never had a childhood.

Among heroines, only Helen's birth is depicted, and it, too, is an abnormal, fantastic one, for she was born from an egg. An Apulian red-figure *pelike* in Kiel from the middle of the fourth century B.C. (Fig. 3, *COA* cat. 7) shows the version of the story that was popular in Athens. Zeus taking the form of a swan mated with Nemesis, who had become a goose in order to avoid Zeus. A shepherd found the egg that she produced from this union and handed it over to Leda. She placed it on a warm altar that eventually caused it to hatch. The moment Helen breaks out of her egg is rendered on the *pelike*. The baby girl reaches out toward Leda, who flees at the unexpected event, while the shepherd stands off to the other side and Eros hovers above.

Female children were not always a welcome addition because the need to supply them with a dowry could place a financial strain on the household. For this reason, they were exposed more often at birth than boys. Exposure, however, was just one of many dangers that children encountered, and once again Greek art usually shows only the mythological gods and heroes facing these dangers, primarily because they are the ones who could most easily overcome them. One exception is the sons and daughters of Niobe, whom Apollo and Artemis slaughtered. Niobe had declared herself more fertile than Leto, the mother of the two gods. This hubristic act caused Leto to complain to her two children, who in turn slaughtered Niobe's seven sons and seven daughters. The massacre is depicted on one of the most famous of all vases, the Niobid Painter's name-piece in the Louvre, a red-figure calyx-krater whose pictures are derived from lost wall-paintings.[2] The myth also occurs on the throne of the great gold and ivory cult statue of Zeus in Olympia made by the famous sculptor Pheidias. These depictions of childhood dangers remind us that the infant mortality rate was much higher in antiquity than today and that many a child died before the age of three.

Fig. 3 (*COA* cat. 7). *The Birth of Helen.* Apulian red-figure *pelike*, attributed to the Painter of Athens 1680, ca. 360–350 B.C. Antikensammlung-Kunsthalle, Kiel (B501)

Childhood

In general, the first six years of a girl's life in ancient Greece were not much different from those of a boy, for both were raised during this phase of their life in the *gynaikeion*, the women's quarter of the house. Mainly their mother, nurses, and female slaves were responsible for their early upbringing, although their father clearly interacted with them as well.

There are a number of household scenes on Greek vases where women interact with children of various ages. Normally, however, when the sex can be determined, the children are boys. An Early Classical red-figure *alabastron* (perfume container) has a riveting picture of a woman with two boys (*COA* cat. 36). She stands with her right hand drawn to her chin, obviously reacting to what she and the boy standing next to her see. He seeks security by grabbing her dress with his left hand, while a younger boy, whom she holds on her left arm, is oblivious to all as he rests his head and arms on her shoulder in a deep, peaceful sleep. It is not clear what has caused her alarm, nor is it certain if she is the children's mother or nurse.

Young girls appear frequently in Greek art in the form of clay figurines. A late-fourth-century B.C. Tanagran terracotta in Boston (Fig. 4, *COA* cat. 40) represents a girl toddler in a particularly active and realistic pose. She sits on the ground and looks up, flailing her arms up and out to either side. This action indicates that she wants to

be picked up. Her chubby, squat proportions accurately reflect those of a pre-toddler, as do her actions, for they are one of the main ways that young children demand attention.

Although they are sad reminders of children who never reached their prime, the Classical gravestones of Athens provide some of the most touching images of young girls. The stele of Melisto, the daughter of Ktesikrates from the *deme* (township) of Potamos, is one of the finest (Fig. 1, *COA* cat. 124). A girl somewhere between six and eight years old stands with her favorite toy and pets: a doll in her left hand, a bird in her right, toward which a Maltese dogs springs. The smile on her face gives no hint of death or sadness; rather the image shows a young, happy child with her playthings—exactly the sort of picture a parent would want when remembering a lost loved one. This child's gravestone and others clearly demonstrate that parents did love their children who had died prematurely for the parents were the ones who chose and paid for the gravestones.

Children also often appear alongside their parents on gravestones. The Athenian stele of Xanthippos of 430–420 B.C. is the most moving of those with girls.[3] The cobbler Xanthippos is shown seated on a *klismos* (backed chair) holding up a shoe last in his right hand.

Fig. 4 (*COA* cat. 40.) *Seated Infant Girl with Outstretched Arms.* Tanagra terracotta figurine, Attic, ca. 330–310 B.C. Museum of Fine Arts, Boston, Anonymous Gift (02.38)

His left hand rests affectionately on the shoulder and back of a young daughter who stands next to him with arms lifted in the air while an older daughter stands by his knees. The latter holds a pet bird in one hand and gestures to him with the other. This portrayal is one of the rare scenes in Greek art in which a father clearly demonstrates his affection for his daughters.

Rarer still are representations of children directly interacting with their grandparents. An absolutely charming early-fifth-century B.C. Boeotian terracotta group shows a seated and balding old man holding out a bunch of grapes to a young girl standing before him, almost certainly his grandchild (*COA* cat. 34). In the other hand he holds a pomegranate, another sweet fruit. We can almost imagine his modern-day counterpart asking, "Would you like some candy or a cookie?"

Fig. 5 (*COA* cat. 77). *Women Spinning Tops.* Attic red-figure squat *lekythos*, ca. 440–430 B.C. The Metropolitan Museum of Art, New York, Gift of Samuel G. Ward, 1875 (75.2.9)

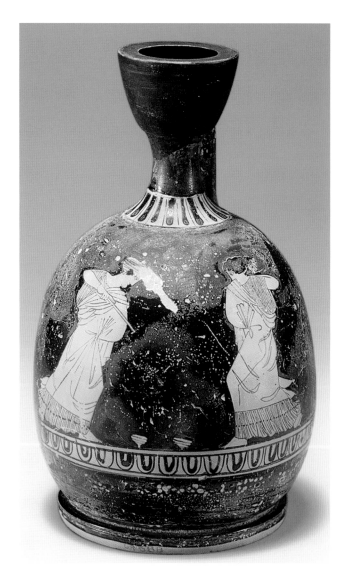

Girls at Play

Play was an essential feature of childhood, and girls are shown either playing alone, among themselves, or with boys, suggesting that brothers and sisters did play together when they were young. Many of the toys that the girls played with are the same as those the boys used, including rollers, balls, and knucklebones. They also both often played with many of the same pets, particularly birds and dogs. On a small red-figure *chous* (pitcher) in Worcester (*COA* cat. 92), for example, a girl in chiton and mantle chases a bird with a toy roller.

Tops are another popular toy that both played with, and a squat *lekythos* in New York (Fig. 5, *COA* cat. 77) shows two females, perhaps a mother and daughter or two girls, actively whipping a pair of tops that spin on the ground between them. The older woman on the left holds her whip at shoulder level, indicating that she has just struck her top with it. The other holds her whip in the same fashion, but most of it is hidden from view by her body. Sometimes tops were placed in children's graves and dedicated at sanctuaries. One in Boston (*COA* cat. 78) is similar to those found dedicated to Pais (literally, "child"), one of the divinities worshiped at the Kabirion, a sanctuary near Thebes. It has a cylindrical body atop a pointed conical base, and black silhouette palmettes and water birds decorate it.

A few toys, such as dolls, were primarily associated with girls. Those with attached limbs, known as articulated dolls, have been found in girls' graves as well as in sanctuaries, thereby indicating they had various functions. The earlier Archaic and Classical ones have legs attached at the hips and their arms are joined at the shoulders. Often, paint indicates their garments, such as the short chiton that is worn by one in New York (Fig. 6, *COA* cat. 73). Starting in the late fifth century a new type of articulated doll develops. The movable parts of the legs now are attached at the knee and the figures are nude, indicating that children placed clothing on them. Many, such as one at Bowdoin College (*COA* cat. 72), can be identified as dancers, because they hold *krotala* (castanets). Many also have a hole at the top of their head where a string was attached, either so that they could be hung as votives or so that the doll could be made to move like a marionette. Gravestones sometimes show girls holding a doll (Fig. 1) as does a white-ground *lekythos*, where a young girl in a chiton brings the toy to the grave.[4]

Greek art shows girls involved in various games, most of which were also played by boys. Based on the number of the depictions known, however, some games seem to have been more for girls than boys. Balancing a stick is one of these. An Attic red-figure *lekythos* in Minneapolis features a well-dressed female who balances a stick on the tips of her fingers (*COA* cat. 80). With the other hand she pulls up on her skirt while going to the right. Agility and control were two obvious requirements for balancing a stick successfully while moving. The age of the female here, as elsewhere, is not possible to ascertain, as artistic convention at this time often did not make a clear distinction between adolescent girls and women.

Juggling was another game favored by girls. Dexterity and hand–eye coordination were qualities developed by this exercise. Females are often shown seated in the *gynaikeion* juggling circular objects, often of uncertain identity. Sometimes they may be apples, but often balls of wool seem to be the best identification because a *kalathos* (wool basket) sits nearby, as seen on a beautiful white-ground *pyxis* (jewelry and cosmetics container) by the Painter of London D 12 (*COA* cat. 81). Both a column and the sandals and wreath hanging in the background indicate an interior setting.

Fig. 6 (*COA* cat. 73). *Doll.*
Corinthian terracotta,
early 5th century B.C.
The Metropolitan Museum of Art,
New York, Rogers Fund, 1944
(44.11.8)

Fig. 7 (*COA* cat. 83).
Girls Playing Ephedrismos.
Hellenistic terracotta
figurine, ca. 300 B.C.
The Metropolitan Museum of Art,
New York, Rogers Fund, 1907
(07.286.4)

Games that both girls and boys frequently are depicted playing include *ephedrismos* and *astragaloi* (knucklebones). Figurines of girls playing *ephedrismos* were particularly popular in the Early Hellenistic period. The goal of this game was to knock over a stone that had been set up by the contestants by throwing balls or pebbles at it. Those who failed to knock it over were required to carry their opponent on their back, with the rider covering her eyes until the stone was knocked over. A beautiful terracotta group in New York (Fig. 7, *COA* cat. 83) shows two young girls playing the game. The carrier holds the rider by her bent right knee, a traditional pose for players, while the rider clings to the carrier's shoulders. The wide splayed legs of both figures indicate rapid motion, and their headdresses suggest that the game may be taking place at a festival.

A terracotta group in Boston (*COA* cat. 85) depicts a pair of crouching female knucklebones players. Various games were played with animal bones. One that ancient art suggests girls particularly liked was *pentelithoi*. Literally "five stones," the game was similar to jacks. The knucklebones were thrown into the air and an attempt was made to catch them on the back of the hand. Those that fell to the ground had to be picked up without dropping the ones that already had been caught on the hand. One of the Boston girls holds a *phormiskos* (carrying sack for bones) in her left hand and reaches to pick up some bones, not shown, with her right hand. The other holds her right arm out, palm down, in the pose used to catch the bones, although again none is visible. These are common poses for knucklebones players, and there is no doubt that the girls are meant to be perceived as playing with these toys.

Boys and girls also played with seesaws, but they are not shown frequently in Greek art. Arguably the finest depiction of a seesaw is found on a column-krater fragment by the Leningrad Painter (Fig. 8, *COA* cat. 82), where two girls play on one. The girl on the right is in midair and about to come down on one end of a plank that is balanced on a log, while the other, standing on the plank's other end, makes ready to be sent aloft. The fruit tree in the background suggests a setting in the countryside rather than in the city.

A Girl's Education and Her Work

Around age seven most Athenian boys went off to school for most of the day. Girls, however, stayed at home, where they learned how to run a household. Cooking was one of these arts, and although in general depictions of girls being taught are rare, a Late Archaic terracotta group in Boston (Fig. 9, *COA* cat. 61) provides a charming picture of a cooking lesson. A woman, seated by a kettle that rests on a tripod above a fire, places herbs or spices into the pot while a young girl looks on. She leans a little too far over the pot, for which reason the woman admonishes her with her left hand, warning her to be careful and draw back.

Fig. 8 (*COA* cat. 82). *Girls on a Seesaw*. Attic red-figure column-krater fragments, attributed to the Leningrad Painter, ca. 470–460 B.C. Museum of Fine Arts, Boston, James Fund and by Special Contribution (10.191a–b)

Fig. 9 (*COA* cat. 61). *Woman Teaching Girl to Cook*. Tanagra terracotta figurine, Boeotian, first quarter of the 5th century B.C. Museum of Fine Arts, Boston, Museum Purchase by Contribution (01.7788)

Pictures of women working wool are common on Attic pottery, and occasionally girls can be distinguished among their numbers. This craft was another one that every mother taught her daughter. An Attic black-figure *lekythos* by the Amasis Painter shows two girls working a loom in the center of a frieze that displays women involved in the various stages of wool-working. One girl moves the shuttle through the standing vertical threads while the other beats the latest woven cord into place with a stick.[5] We also see girls on Attic vases, particularly black-figure *hydriai*, fetching water from the fountain house, although their social status is unclear and debated.[6] And some girls are shown performing other household chores, including child care.[7]

Although most girls did not go to school, there is clear evidence that some women did read and write. Most likely, they learned these skills while at home. An Attic red-figure cup of about 460 B.C. in New York (Fig. 10, *COA* cat. 46) has an intriguing scene in its tondo that at first glance suggests otherwise. A woman leads by the wrist another who holds a writing case with a stylus in her right hand. The picture is reminiscent of other scenes that show boys going off to school with their *paidagogoi*, so that some scholars have thought that this girl, contrary to what the literary evidence suggests is the norm, is going off to school. The pictures on the outside of the cup help explain this apparent contradiction of evidence. There, among the objects hanging in the background between the six conversing women on each side, are two pairs of *krotala* (castanets). Traditionally courtesans used these clappers when dancing for their customers, thereby indicating that

the women on this vase are *hetairai*, female companions, some of whom did learn their letters in order to be better able to entertain their male customers at the symposium, the main occasion when such drinking cups were used. The scene then is an appropriate one for the type of vessel on which it is found.

Pictures of young girls training also are known. On an Attic red-figure *lekythos* by the Phiale Painter (Fig. 11, *COA* cat. 58) a dancing girl practices before an instructor. The girl's hair is tied in back, and she is nude, except for the cross-girt apparatus across her chest. Her mistress guides the girl's movements with her right hand and holds a staff, or *narthex*, in her left hand, an instrument that the literary sources tell us was used to beat out the rhythm of the dance and to enforce discipline. These dancing girls were normally either slaves or children from the lower classes, and several vase-paintings show them entertaining men.

Fig. 10 (*COA* cat. 46.) *Girls Going to School(?)*. Attic red-figure *kylix*, attributed to the Painter of Bologna 417, ca. 460 B.C. The Metropolitan Museum of Art, New York, Rogers Fund, 1906 (06.1021.167)

Fig. 11 (*COA* cat. 58). *Girl Learning to Dance*. Attic red-figure *lekythos*, attributed to the Phiale Painter, ca. 440–435 B.C. Bowdoin College Museum of Art, Brunswick, Maine, Gift of Edward Perry Warren, Esq., Honorary Degree, 1926 (1913.011)

Scenes such as these remind us that many girls did not live the privileged life of an Athenian citizen. In fact, many slave girls often were forced from an early age to do hard manual labor. Such is the case with the young girl depicted on an Attic red-figure *skyphos* in Malibu (Fig. 12, *COA* cat. 63). While her mistress greedily gulps down the contents of a drinking cup, the slave girl stands by fully laden with cargo: she has a full wineskin on her head and holds a sack over her shoulder with one hand and a pot down in the other hand—a very heavy load for one so small. Slave girls are also shown helping out with household chores such as child care and carrying various objects during a visit to a tomb.[8]

Girls of the lower class also often had to do manual labor by helping out in the fields or by bringing the agricultural products to market. A number of vases depict girls helping women pick fruit. These pictures, however, often have been thought to be connected with ritual rather than work.[9]

Older aristocratic girls could become *kanephoroi*, virgins who were chosen to carry a sacrificial basket. A terracotta figurine in Amsterdam (Fig. 13, *COA* cat. 108) shows four of them in a row, although only traces of the one at the right remain. Dressed in a *peplos*, each carries a *kanoun* (sacrificial basket) on top of her head. The contents of the one on the left is visible—barley used to attract the sacrificial animal to the altar. *Kanephoroi* are also pictured in vase-paintings as part of the procession to the altar as well as on the Parthenon's east frieze.

Other terracotta figurines present girls who are dressed for festive occasions, although we often do not know exactly for which ritual. A seated girl with tambourine and wreath (*COA* cat. 109) whose hair is carefully arranged in the style known as *lampadion*, or "little torch," because it resembles the flames of a torch, may be dressed for a festival for Dionysos or Cybele. Also clothed for a festival is a girl on an Attic red-figure *lekythos* by the Brygos Painter.[11]

Fig. 12 (*COA* cat. 63). *Young Slave Girl with Mistress*. Attic red-figure *skyphos*, ca. 470–460 B.C. The J. Paul Getty Museum, Malibu, California (86.AE.265)

Fig. 13 (*COA* cat. 108). *Four Kanephoroi*. Tarantine mold-made figurine, ca. 450–425 B.C. Allard Pierson Museum, Amsterdam (1159)

Girls and Ritual

Although girls spent most of their time at home, participation in various rituals provided an opportunity for them to appear in public. As we have already seen, girls are depicted on *choes*, small pitchers thought to have been given to children at the Anthesteria, possibly for their first sip of wine. Besides playing, the girls sometimes are shown carrying ritual cakes. On one *chous* found in the Athenian Agora a young girl decked out in a chiton and *ependytes*, one's Sunday best, moves speedily to the right carrying an *omphalos* cake while accompanied by her pet Maltese dog.[10] Frolicking boys are shown to either side of her.

She holds sprigs in both hands, and a woman behind, probably a *metic* (resident alien), protects her from the sun by holding a parasol over her head.

Pictures of girls actively participating in festivals also exist. A series of Archaic Corinthian vases shows women along with girls taking part in all-female rituals, possibly connected with the goddess Artemis in her role as protector of young children. A good example is a bottle in London of 625–600 B.C. on which women and young girls walk in procession with an adolescent girl carrying a ritual basket laden with vases atop her head.[12]

Girls also are shown on Attic pottery participating in a festival to honor Artemis, the Arkteia. The foundation story for this ritual relates how a young girl teased a tame bear that lived in the Attic sanctuary of Artemis at Brauron. The bear scratched her, drawing blood, whereupon several boys who were with the girls murdered the bear. Artemis was angered that the animal was killed in her sanctuary, so as recompense she ordered that young girls must serve her as "Little Bears."

Although we do not know the exact nature of the ritual, we do know that a number of preadolescent girls were chosen every four years to live in the goddess's sanctuary at Brauron to serve as "Little Bears" and that during the festival they would "play the bear." A series of fifth-century B.C. *krateriskoi*, small kraters in the form of chalices, preserve scenes apparently connected with this rite.[13] On them long-haired girls, either nude or dressed in a short tunic, hold torches or twigs and run in the presence of altars, palms, and priestesses or marshals. Once, even a bear is shown. It is not clear if the girls are running in a race at the sanctuary or "playing the bear." Apparently, the wearing or shedding of a saffron robe was also part of the ritual. After the girls completed their service in the sanctuary, they were deemed ready for marriage. A number of charming fourth-century statues of both boys and girls also have been found at Brauron that are probably offerings to Artemis for a successful childbirth.[14]

Several other Attic vases show a girl on a swing in the company of men, the most famous one being the name-piece of the Attic black-figure artist the Swing Painter.[15] The scenes on these vessels are thought to be connected with the Aiora, an Athenian rite performed at the Anthesteria that involved young girls swinging in order to appease the ghost of Erigone. She hung herself in sorrow at the death of her father, Ikarios, who, after introducing viticulture to Athens, was murdered by drunken men because they thought that they had been poisoned. Erigone's death set off a slew of similar suicides by young women. The establishment of this expiatory rite meant that people could honor Erigone by swinging in a manner similar to hanging but without the deadly result. An Apulian red-figure *lekythos* in New York (*COA* cat. 102) shows a woman pushing a young girl on a swing; both are in festive dress and in the company of Hermes and a boy seated on an altar. The column and the altar indicate a sanctuary setting, suggesting that a similar rite was practiced in southern Italy, since the vase was made there.

Children also participated in family rituals, such as marriages and funerals. We see girls, for example, taking part in the *loutrophoreia*, the procession to gather the water for the bridal bath that took place on the night before the *gamos* (wedding) proper. On a red-figure *loutrophoros* by the Pan Painter (Fig. 14, *COA* cat. 110) a boy playing the *aulos* (double-flute) leads the procession.

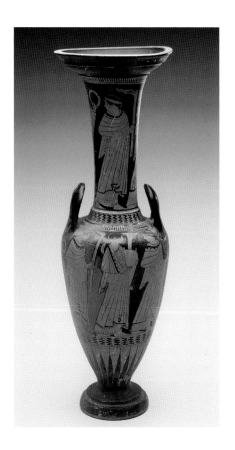
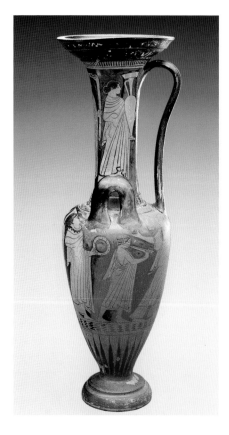

Fig. 14 (*COA* cat. 110). *Preparations for the Bride's Wedding Bath*. Attic red-figure *loutrophoros-hydria*, attributed to the Pan Painter, ca. 470 B.C. The Museum of Fine Arts, Houston, Gift of Miss Annette Finnigan (37.10)

The second figure behind him is the bride, who carries a *loutrophoros*, the special vase used to carry the bridal bath water. It was also placed on the tombs of those who had died unmarried. The torch held by the woman behind the bride indicates that the procession takes place at night. A girl holding a wreath follows her. The bath was thought to purify the bride and increase fertility.

Care of the dead was primarily women's work, and girls, even at an early age, took part in the various stages of the funeral. Already on Archaic Attic black-figure vases they are shown at the *prothesis* (the lying-in-state). An early-fifth-century black-figure *pinax* (plaque) in Paris by the Sappho Painter has a complex picture of this event. Two girls are shown on it, one of whom is labeled "sister."[16] Other family members also are identified, and both girls mourn, as do the other women surrounding the bier, either with one hand to the head and the other out or with both hands to the head.

The most popular fifth-century funerary scene, the visit to the grave, decorates primarily Attic white-ground *lekythoi*. These special Athenian vessels were placed in and on Athenian graves and were put around the bier at the *prothesis*. A number show girls at the grave. One in Malibu by the Painter of Athens 1826 (*COA* cat. 113) has a young girl and boy by the tomb. The girl offers a flower with one hand and holds an *alabastron* with the other. The boy stands on the other side of the grave and puts a fillet around the stele that stands in the middle of the picture behind a *tymbos*, the mound of dirt marking the grave. The white coloring both the girl's skin and the tomb is a common feature on the early white *lekythoi*. Periodic visits to the grave and its upkeep were a woman's responsibility, which young girls learned early.

The Transition to Womanhood

Marriage and the birth of a child marked the official end of a girl's childhood, which was often much shorter than a boy's, for she married at a much younger age. Aristotle suggests eighteen as the appropriate age for females and thirty-seven for males [*Politics* 1335a28–29]. Bridal preparations are shown on numerous vase-paintings, such as a those on a *lebes gamikos*—wedding bowl—in Mississippi, an appropriate scene for this type of vessel (*COA* cat. 128). On one side, we see the seated bride among her companions looking at herself in a mirror. The woman behind her may be the *nympheutria*, her main assistant, and the girl before her a sister. On the other side of the bowl, a seated bride holds a small wooden chest that she may have just received as part of the gifts given to her on the Epaulia, the day after the wedding night, when her family and friends visited her in her new home

to witness that she had safely survived the transition. Meanwhile, a mythological scene runs around the base: Peleus' pursuit of the sea nymph Thetis. They will eventually marry and produce Achilles, the greatest of Greek heroes. This pursuit scene is best perceived as a metaphor for courtship, so that the vase shows three moments: the courtship, the preparations for the wedding, and the day after the wedding, when the girl has become a woman ensconced in her new home.

Greek art, then, provides us with a rich tableau of childhood images of girls, from birth to their coming of age. It provides clear evidence that many daughters were loved by their parents and that girls, like boys, played important roles in both Greek family and civic life. In addition, a viewer cannot help but be struck by how keenly aware the Greek artists were of their young subjects, for they depicted the girls' gestures, poses, and interests with remarkable accuracy. One cannot help but conclude that these representations truly are worthy of being deemed part of "The Greek Miracle."

NOTES

1. Cyprus Museum, Nicosia (B 56); Lewis 2002, 15, figs. 1, 2; Dierichs 2002, pl. 4.

2. Musée du Louvre, Paris (G 341): *COA* 118, fig. 6.

3. British Museum, London (1805.7-3.183): *COA* 184, fig. 25.

4. Private collection: *COA* 168, fig. 8.

5. Metropolitan Museum of Art, New York (31.11.10): *COA* 151, fig. 10.

6. Lewis 2002, 1–4, 71–75, fig. 2.15, for example.

7. Ibid., 81, fig. 2.25, for example.

8. Ibid., 17, fig. 1.4, for example, and 2835; *COA* 172 and 301–2, cat. 116.

9. Ibid., 26, fig. 1.12.

10. Agora Museum, Athens (P7685): *COA* 147, fig. 7.

11. Museo Archeologico, Paestum: *COA* 18, fig. 2.

12. Lewis 2002, 49, fig. 1.30.

13. *COA* 151–52, fig. 11; Reeder 1995, 321–28.

14. For example, *COA* 152, fig. 12.

15. Museum of Fine Arts, Boston (98.918): *COA* 149, fig. 8.

16. Musée du Louvre, Paris (MNB 905): *COA* 165, fig. 3.

But like some young sapling in an orchard was Herakles nurtured at his mother's side. . . .

Letters old Linos taught the boy, Apollo's heroic son, his watchful guardian.

To bend a bow and loose an arrow at the target Eurytios . . . taught him.

Eumolpos made him a bard and formed his two hands on the lyre of boxwood.

All the tricks whereby the hip-twisting men of Argos throw each other with their legs,

All the devices which boxers skilled in their thongs of leather, all that pankratists

Who throw themselves to the ground have devised in furtherance of their art,

He learnt in tutelage to Hermes' son Harpalykos. . . .

To drive forth his horses in the chariot Amphitryon himself taught his son with loving care.

How with spear couched to keep his shoulder behind his shield and tilt at his man,

How to abide the strokes of swords . . . all this he learned from Kastor, son of Hippalos. . . .

Such was the schooling his dear mother found for Herakles.

—Theokritos 24: 103–36

Fig. 15 (COA cat. 1). *Young Boy.* Pentelic marble statue,
Late Hellenistic, ca. 100 B.C.–A.D. 100.
Virginia Museum of Fine Arts, Richmond,
The Adolph D. and Wilkins C. Williams Fund
(89.24a/b)

A BOY'S LIFE IN ANCIENT GREECE

Jenifer Neils

This poem by the third-century B.C. Alexandrian poet Theokritos describing the mythical boyhood of the young Herakles serves as a curriculum vitae of any young aristocratic boy of the period. Reading and writing, music, athletics, horsemanship, and the arts of warfare were all standard requirements for boys in ancient Greece, and special education teachers were also the norm. The hero Herakles naturally was tutored by the best the world could offer, but even mortal youths received instruction from skilled practitioners. Just as boys today desire to grow up to be superheroes or football stars, so in antiquity mythological champions like Herakles, Theseus, and Achilles served as models for young males. In examining the typical life of the Greek boy, one can see how the idyll about Herakles strikes a familiar note.

Fig. 16 (COA cat. 29). *Household Family Scene*. Attic red-figure *hydria*, attributed to the Circle of Polygnotos, ca. 440–430 B.C. Harvard University Art Museums, Arthur M. Sackler Museum, Cambridge, Bequest of David Moore Robinson (1960.342)

Fig. 17 (RIGHT) (COA cat. 6). *Birth of Erichthonios*. Attic red-figure calyx-krater, attributed to the Nikias Painter, ca. 410 B.C. Virginia Museum of Fine Arts, Richmond, The Arthur and Margaret Glasgow Fund (81.70)

Infancy and Early Childhood

In ancient Greece, male children were favored from birth, and so they were less likely to be exposed than girls. In a play by Euripides, Iphigeneia states that the "pillars of the house are the male children" (*Iphigeneia in Tauris* 57), reflecting a commonly held belief. When a male infant was born in Athens a wreath of olive was posted on the door of the house to announce his successful delivery. Since this was also the victory crown at the Olympics, it may suggest the hope that the newborn would grow up to be as healthy and strong as an Olympic athlete. In well-to-do households the infant would have been turned over to a wet nurse for care and feeding. On a fifth-century Athenian vase (Fig. 16, *COA* cat. 29) we see both the transfer of the male baby and the olive wreath hanging directly over it. The new mother sits in the center on a chair known as a *klismos* while her youthful, presumably proud, husband stands behind her. The center of attention is the nude infant, clearly shown as male, who reaches out to his nurse who is identifiable as such by her sleeved garment. The baby is protected by the typical string of apotropaic amulets worn across his chest.

This scene is echoed by one on an Athenian vase painted about thirty years later (Fig. 17, *COA* cat. 6).

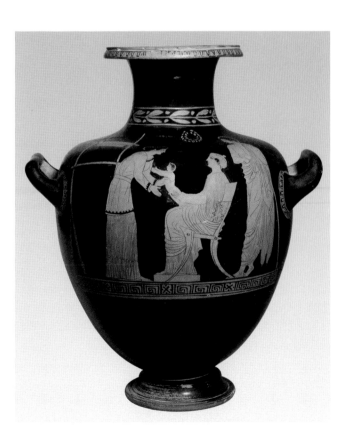

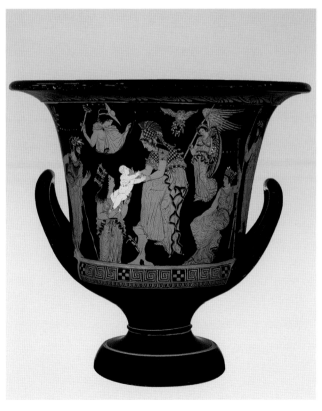

Again a male baby wearing a string of amulets is being handed from one woman to another and an olive wreath is depicted above, held in the talons of a flying owl. But in this case the mother is the earth goddesses Ge or Gaia and the "nurse" is none other than the patron deity of Athens, Athena. This scene is the birth of the future Athenian king Erichthonios, the result of the smith-god Hephaistos' failed attempt on the virtue of Athena. Hephaistos stands behind Ge, looking on but removed from the action just like the father on the earlier hydria (Fig. 16, *COA* cat. 29). Other deities have assembled to witness the birth: Hermes with his traveler's cap and *kerykeion*, winged Nike holding Athena's shield and spear, a seated Aphrodite, and the grandfather Zeus behind her. Although the setting is outdoors and not a domestic interior, it is remarkable how similar real-life and mythological depictions can be.

Fig. 18 (*COA* cat. 20). *Gravestone with Woman and Infant.* Attic marble grave stele, ca. 375–350 B.C. The Museum of Fine Arts, Houston, Gift of Miss Annette Finnigan (37.25)

Many rituals attended the birth of a male child, according to our sources which describe primarily Athenian rites. About the fifth day after birth, the Amphidromia signaled the newborn's acceptance into the family. In this ritual the father carried the infant at a run around the domestic hearth, followed by feasting. On the tenth day the newborn was given his name, usually that of his paternal grandfather if he was the firstborn son. In the autumn after the child's birth he was officially introduced to his father's *phratry*, or brotherhood, an age-old hereditary association of all Ionian Greeks. After swearing to the legitimacy of his child, the father presented an animal for sacrifice. At the age of three Athenian children were given their first taste of wine at the festival of Dionysos known as the Anthesteria. A souvenir of the festival, a miniature wine jug known as a *chous*, was presumably given to children as they are often found in children's graves. These *choes* (see figs. 25, 26) preserve some of the most charming illustrations of childhood (or what their adult makers thought of it), and in many cases the age of the child, primarily male, is directly related to the size of the *chous*. All these Athenian religious rituals were no doubt conducted in order to ensure the male child's future success in his father's world.

Because of the more primitive state of medicine and sanitation in ancient times, new mothers and their offspring were especially susceptible to illness and death. Many young mothers-to-be died in childbirth, and this common fate resonates in many myths, such as that of Semele, who was immolated when she was impregnated by Zeus. A number of finely carved marble grave stelai from the region of Athens commemorate mothers who died during or just after giving birth. The preserved upper half of one in Houston (Fig. 18, *COA* cat. 20) shows the mother with bowed head at the left and the nursemaid at the right holding the swaddled newborn. In mythological scenes, one is more likely to see the messenger god Hermes ferrying the newborn to its care-giver, as in the case of Dionysos, son of Zeus and Semele, whom Hermes is often shown carrying to the nymphs of Mount Nysa—notably in the famous statue by Praxiteles found at Olympia. Arkas, who gave his name to the region of Arkadia, is another orphaned male infant; he was the son of Zeus and Kallisto, who was transformed by jealous Hera into a bear after she gave birth. On a fourth-century silver coin of Pheneos, Hermes is shown dashing to the left with the baby Arkas cradled on his left arm (*COA* cat. 9) en route to the god's mother, Maia, who will care for the abandoned child.

Motherless or not, mythological babies often reveal signs of their future heroism. Herakles is the most precocious; as an infant he strangled two poisonous snakes sent by the ever-jealous Hera (Fig. 19, *COA* cats. 11, 12). Perseus, set adrift at sea in a wooden box with his mother, Danae, survived and grew up to become the beheader of the gorgon Medusa. He is shown as a helpless infant reaching toward his mother on a beautiful early-fifth-century Athenian *lekythos* (*COA* cat. 13), and the funerary associations of this vase shape, a flask for perfumed oil given to the dead, reinforce the lugubrious fortune awaiting the infant. Another whose life was threatened at an early age is the hero Orestes, son of Agamemnon and Clytemnestra. On a large krater from south Italy (*COA* cat. 17 reverse) he is shown in the clutches of the wounded warrior Telephos, who vows to kill him at the blood-stained altar if his parents do not reveal the secret to his cure.

As we know, he survived to avenge his father's murder, but on the other side of this impressive vase (Fig. 20, *COA* cat. 17 obverse) we encounter two boys who did not. Their limp corpses draped over a long altar, these sons of Medea and Jason are the unfortunate victims of a mother's embittered rage against an unfaithful husband. While Jason rails at Medea, she flies off in her magnificent snake-drawn chariot encircled by a radiant nimbus. The only mourners for the dead brothers are their old Thracian nurse and their *paidagogos*, or male tutor. With her white hair and tattooed arms, the nurse collapses with grief at the altar. More restrained in his mourning is the balding tutor, who stands holding one hand to his head in the typical male gesture of bereavement. This vase is unique in representing two scenes of children, both of which are illustrations of plays by the tragedian Euripides *Telephos* and *Medea*.

Fig. 19 (*COA* cat. 11). *Herakles Strangling the Snakes.*
Silver stater from Croton, Bruttium, mid-4th century B.C.
The American Numismatic Society, New York
(1955.54.42)

Fig. 20 (*COA* cat. 17). *Medea Escaping in Her Chariot.*
Lucanian red-figure calyx-krater, attributed to near the Policoro Painter, ca. 400 B.C. The Cleveland Museum of Art, Leonard C. Hanna, Jr., Fund (1991.1)

Schooling for Boys

The figure of the *paidagogos*, as seen on the Medea krater and as portrayed in numerous terracotta figurines (such as *COA* cat. 47), was the first and most important mentor in a younger boy's life. He was generally a household slave who looked after small boys until they reached school age and then accompanied them to their special tutors outside the home beginning at about the age of seven. He is often depicted in later Greek art as an elderly, paunchy, bearded, snub-nosed man—not unlike a satyr or silen. In fact, statuettes of a child with his *paidagogos* look remarkably like those of Papposilenos with his charge, the toddler Dionysos (*COA* cat. 8). These male role models served as substitutes for the absentee father who spent much of his time away from the household. But the best tutor a young hero could hope for would be a wise old centaur like Chiron. This half-human half-equine creature served as *paidagogos* for many a Greek hero, the most famous being Achilles, who is shown on numerous vases (for example, *COA* cat. 14) as he is turned over to Chiron by his father, Peleus. Because of his hybrid form, a centaur was ideally suited to teach riding as well as the usual subjects for a young hero: reading and writing, music, athletics, and hunting.

Fig. 21 (*COA* cat. 43). *Boy at Shoemaker's.* Attic black-figure *pelike*, attributed to the Eucharides Painter, ca. 500 B.C. The University of Oxford, Oxford, Ashmolean Museum (G 247)

Boys emerged from the *oikos* and attended school at about the age of seven. For these daily trips outside the home they would need, for the first time, a pair of shoes or sandals. A famous Athenian black-figure vase in Oxford (Fig. 21, *COA* cat. 43) provides a glimpse into the shoemaker's shop, of which there were probably many in the vicinity of the ancient Agora, just as today one can find sandal makers in the Plaka. The boy stands on a table while the cobbler cuts a piece of leather to the size of his foot. To steady himself the child places his right hand on the shoemaker's bent head. Standing and watching at the right is either the boy's father or his *paidagogos*. The setting is indicated by the tools hanging on the wall and the basin for softening leather beneath the table. Such touching genre scenes involving young children are rare in Greek art, and this vase may thus have been a special commission.

Once at school a boy encountered the *grammatistes*, who taught reading and writing. The first task of a schoolboy was to learn to write the alphabet forward and backward. The trial piece of a boy named Kametis, a broken bit of pottery (*COA* cat. 51), shows that he could write his name and the first four letters of the Greek alphabet but then got flummoxed when trying to render them in reverse. Next came the memorization of syllables, as can be seen in neat columns on a whitewashed wooden board from Egypt (*COA* cat. 52). Finally, the student learned to copy entire passages, such as hexameters from Greek poetry, as shown on a papyrus fragment, also from Egypt (*COA* cat. 53). In these exercises the student used ink on a variety of media: cheap pot shards, wooden boards, and more expensive papyrus. His ink (*melan*) was derived from burned pine-pitch resin and was stored in ceramic inkwells, one of which takes the familiar form of a stitched leather ball, not unlike our soccer ball (*COA* cat. 50). Another medium for writing—one that could be conveniently reused—was the wax tablet and stylus (*COA* cat. 49). In the tondo of an Athenian wine cup (Fig. 22, *COA* cat. 48) we see a schoolboy hard at work, using his stylus to incise letters into his open wax tablet (that just coincidently looks like today's laptop computer).

The second of the boy's three special education teachers was the *kitharistes*, or music teacher. According to Plato (*Protagoras* 326 A), "the *kitharistes* teaches the boys to play the lyre and then to sing lyric songs to their own accompaniment. In this way they become more cultured, more controlled and better balanced people, and their behavior is all the better for it." An Athenian red-figure wine cup illustrates what might be a young boy with his music teacher (*COA* cat. 45). He stands demurely holding his tortoiseshell lyre while the older man gazes down at him. An older boy with his (stringless) lyre is shown in a sanctuary setting in the tondo of another cup (*COA* cat. 104), perhaps dedicating his instrument to the god of music Apollo. Both boys seem very well behaved and so Plato's dictum regarding the good effects of musical training may have held true.

The third essential area of a boy's education was athletics, and for this he went to the palaistra to train under the direction of a *paidotribes*. These young athletes and their trainers were a popular subject for late-sixth- and early-fifth-century Athenian vase painters (see cats. B, C, D). One of the more admired athletes was one who competed in the pentathlon because he needed an array of skills to be victorious. The interior of a *kylix* in the Hood Museum (Fig. 23, COA cat. 55) shows a young pentathlete preparing for another event, boxing. The ground of the palaistra is littered with his equipment: a large discus, two black jumping weights (*halteres*), and a pick for loosening the ground to make a soft landing for the jump. In the background hangs his hygiene equipment: sponge, strigil, and round *aryballos* for oil. The youth is in the process of tightening the leather strap that he has wrapped around his palm and wrist for protection during boxing. An image of two children boxing can be found on a small *chous* (COA cat. 54); these nude, wreathed boys may be competing in a boxing contest held in conjunction with the Anthesteria. They are flanked by two turn posts that were used for long-distance races.

Fig. 22 (*COA* cat. 48). *Youth Writing*. Attic red-figure *kylix*, attributed to the Eucharides Painter, ca. 480 B.C. University of Pennsylvania, Philadelphia, Museum of Archaeology and Anthropology (MS 4842)

Fig. 23 (*COA* cat. 55). *Athlete*. Attic red-figure *kylix*, attributed to the Epidromos Painter, ca. 520–500 B.C. Dartmouth College, Hood Museum of Art, Hanover, N.H., Gift of Mr. and Mrs. Ray Winfield Smith, Class of 1918 (C.1970.35)

Another area in which boys may have trained under adult male supervision is at religious rituals and major festivals. We know, for instance, that it was the custom for a *pais amphithaleis* (boy with both parents living) to cut with a golden sickle the olive branches from the sacred tree at Olympia for the victory crowns. A young boy is depicted on the east frieze of the Parthenon helping the chief priest fold the newly woven *peplos* that was presented to the goddess Athena every four years at her festival, the Great Panathenaia. In Athenian vase paintings and relief sculpture a boy is often shown assisting the older priest in animal sacrifice, leading the sacrificial victim to the altar. In the interior of a red-figure cup (*COA* cat. 105) a boy carries a *kanoun* (basket) in one hand and a piglet by the rear leg in another. Pigs were traditionally sacrificed to

Fig. 24 (*COA* cat. 106). *Sacrifice Scene*. Attic red-figure neck-amphora, attributed to the Niobid Painter, ca. 460 B.C. Brooklyn Museum of Art, Museum Collection Fund (59.34)

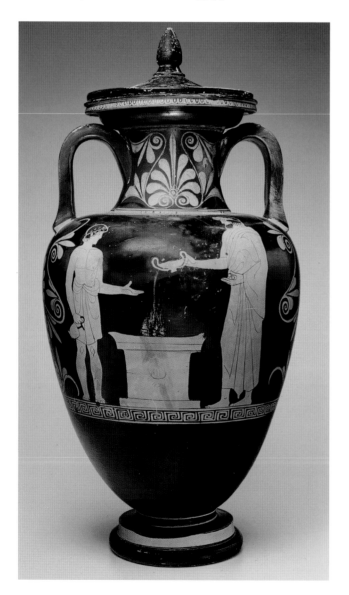

the grain goddess Demeter. On an amphora in Brooklyn (Fig. 24, *COA* cat. 106) a young acolyte is holding the wine jug while the priest pours wine from a *kantharos* onto a flaming altar, perhaps an offering to Dionysos. Boys also helped warriors perform a rite of augury known as *extispicy*, in which the liver of an animal was examined for clues to the outcome of the battle. An undefiled or pure boy was the most auspicious person to hold the entrails so they would not be tainted before divination.

The curriculum outlined above was that of well-to-do Athenian boys whose fathers could afford to hire special teachers. In Sparta, fathers had little input into their sons' education because it was regulated by the state under the auspices of a special official called the *paidonomos* ("boy herdsman"). From the age of seven, Spartan youth spent their time in military and athletic training and lived and dined apart from their parents with their age cohort. This system of public upbringing known as the *agoge* was intended to inculcate conformity and loyalty to the state. The poorer children in any state were apprenticed at an early age to craftsmen or worked alongside their farmer parents in the fields. Slave children were common in ancient Greece, and they were almost certainly overworked and underfed.

Boys' Entertainments

Life for boys in ancient Greece was, however, not all work and schooling; they had many diversions in the form of toys, games, and pets. Male toddlers are almost invariably shown with their rollers or toy carts, especially on Attic *choes* (Fig. 25, *COA* cat. 91) and grave stelai. Made of wood and called a *hamax* according to Aristophanes (*Clouds* 879–80), the toy consisted of a stick attached to an axle with two wheels, between which a box could be placed for transporting objects like *choes*, pet animals, or one's playmates. As a boy grew older he might acquire a hoop (*COA* cat. 76) and a rod to trundle it along. In Attic vase painting the hoop becomes the standard attribute of the handsome young Trojan prince Ganymede, who is taken to Mount Olympus by Zeus to become the cup-bearer of the gods. Another toy beloved of Greek boys (and girls) was the top, or *strobilos*, which was set spinning with a whip. It has been suggested that the god Hermes invented the spinning top, so it is not surprising to see him represented on an Athenian cup playing with one (*COA* cat. 16). He is watching the large top intently as his young male companion seems to be exclaiming over the endurance of its spin.

Clearly another favorite pastime was pets. The youngest children are regularly depicted with their birds (Fig. 25, *COA* cat. 91). Many vase paintings show various species of birds in the domestic quarters of the household, where boys dwelled until they went to school. Older boys are shown playing with their dogs (*COA* cat. 95) or exotic cats (*COA* cat. 93), teaching them tricks with a piece of meat as an enticement. The little dog jumps for it while the cat climbs nimbly up the boy's walking stick. Perhaps as preparation for chariot racing, little boys had small carts propelled by goats. Mimicking adult behavior even to the long charioteer's gown and the *kentron*, or goad, a little boy whips his domesticated goats into a gallop on a small, colorful *chous* (*COA* cat. 99).

At a later age boys took part in interactive games, many of which involved a ball. The game of *passe-boule* that is depicted on a medium-size chous (*COA* cat. 79)

shows one boy pitching a ball at a stick planted in the ground. Another boy beyond the wicket is awaiting the throw. Possibly the best-loved game of boys involved *astragaloi*, or knucklebones (*COA* cats. 88, 90), as evidenced by the large number found in graves. These asymmetrical anklebones of sheep or goats could land on one of four sides that were assigned numerical values, like dice. They were carried around like our marbles in leather bags, which are often shown clutched in the hands of children or hanging in the background of a vase painting (cf. *COA* cat. 104 above). A larger *chous* (Fig. 26, *COA* cat. 86) shows three boys crouching on the ground intent in their game of knucklebones. Apparently, children were fiercely possessive of their *astragaloi*, for the *Iliad* (23.88) tells of the Greek warrior Patroklos losing at knucklebones as a child and becoming so enraged that he killed his playmate.

Fig. 25 (*COA* cat. 91). *Boy with His Pet Bird*. Attic red-figure *chous*, ca. 425–420 B.C. Museum of Fine Arts, Boston, Henry Lillie Pierce Fund (01.8086)

Fig. 26 (*COA* cat. 86). *Boys Playing Knucklebones*. Attic red-figure *chous*, attributed to the Group of Boston 10.190, ca. 420 B.C. The J. Paul Getty Museum, Malibu, California (96.AE.28)

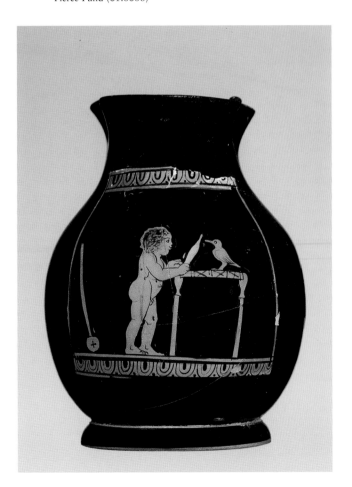

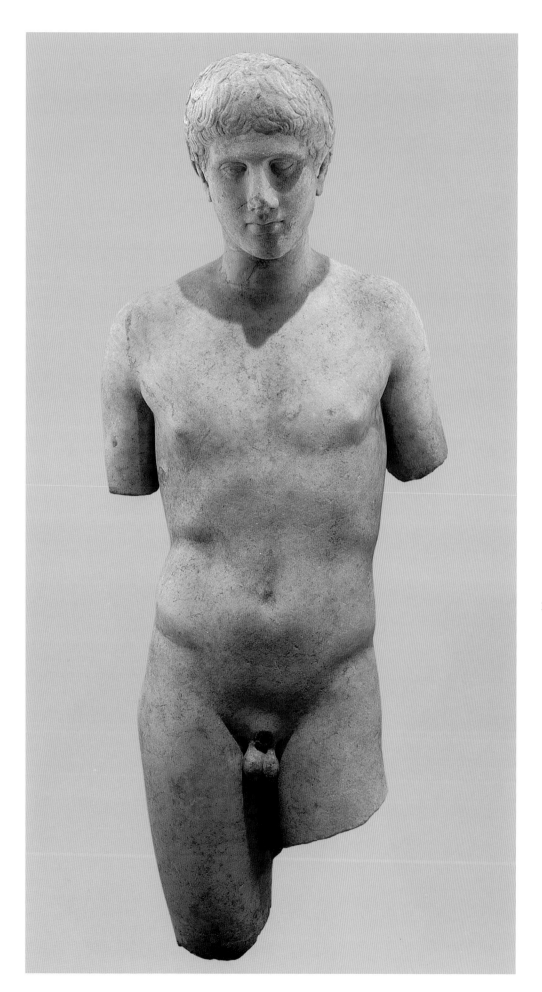

Fig. 27 (COA cat. 127).
          Youth. Marble statue,
          Roman copy of a Greek
          original of ca. 430 B.C.
          Carnegie Museum of Art,
          Pittsburgh, AODA
          Purchase Fund, 1971
          (71.16)

Coming of Age

At some point during his adolescence a Greek boy had to give up childish things. This transition was marked by the symbolic act of dedicating his playthings to a male deity. A third-century verse tells of one Philokles performing this ritual:

> To Hermes, Philokles here hangs up these toys of
> his boyhood;
> His noiseless ball, this lively boxwood rattle, his
> knucklebones
> He had such a mania for, and his spinning top.

At age sixteen, about the age of the handsome youth in Pittsburgh (Fig. 27, *COA* cat. 127), an Athenian male was officially enrolled in his father's phratry, where he had been introduced within a year of his birth. This act was accompanied by an official hair-cutting ritual known as the *koureion*. At age eighteen he became an Athenian citizen, acquiring voting rights and civic obligations. At this point he left his family and lived with his peers, fulfilling two years of military service as an *ephebe*. Very different from an Athenian girl who married in her early adolescence, an Athenian boy enjoyed an extended period during which he was prepared to take on the public responsibilities of his adult life.

The road traveled from childhood (Fig. 15, *COA* cat. 1) to the brink of manhood by the ancient Greek male would not be unfamiliar to a boy today, consisting as it did of nurture by females, play, schooling, religious service, and athletics. Much of what we consider good child rearing was already practiced by elite families in ancient Greece, although the female half of the population was excluded and the father's engagement was more limited. And much of what we now glean about the lives of boys in ancient Greece comes from charming images painted on vases or sculpted in marble as well as from their personal possessions recovered through archaeology. Although children have often been called the "invisible" people of the past, it is clear from the artistic evidence that they played a central role then as they do today.

You say, "I want to win at Olympia." But wait. Look at what is involved. . . .
You will have to obey instructions, keep away from desserts,
eat only at set hours, in both heat and cold;
you must not drink cold water nor can you have a drink of wine whenever you want.
You must hand yourself over to your coach exactly as you would to a doctor.
Then in the contest you must gouge and be gouged; there will be times when
you will sprain a wrist, twist your ankle, swallow mouthfuls of sand and be flogged.
And after all that there are times when you will lose.

—Epiktetos, *Discourses* 15.2–5

YOUNG GREEK ATHLETES

Christine Kondoleon

If we had to select a figural icon for ancient Greece, it might well be the white marble statues of perfectly formed nude young men, kouroi. The proliferation of these statues dedicated to Apollo in the Archaic period expresses an essential cultural value, the ideal of *kalokagathia* ("the beautiful and the good"), or physical and moral excellence. The presentation of these young men as nude, *gymnos*, is of signal importance because it associates them with athletes. Many kouroi represent the sons of the elite class of male citizens for whom the rigorous training and competition of Greek athletics was required. Indeed, one key rite of passage from *pais* into *aner*, from boy to man, was through athletic training. Nudity might also be read as a costume in the sense of what was worn for an initiation. The nude public male figure then is a multivalent symbol of a Greek ideal, of a ritual, and of actual training and competition.[1]

Parents wanted their daughters to marry early, about fourteen, and to bear children. Their ambition for their sons, however, is more challenging to translate into modern terms. It involved the attainment of manly qualities (*andreia*)—simply stated, courage and virtue. Outside of war, the most public forum for manly displays was the festival games held throughout the Greek-speaking world. The training for these competitions was conducted within the precincts of the palaistra-gymnasion complexes that could be found in most Greek towns and cities. It was here that young males in their teenage years were taught music, philosophy, and gymnastics.[2] They perfected their bodies and built up their endurance under the watchful eyes of their physical trainers, or *paidotribes*. During the sixth century there was an increase in the construction of gymnasia, making this type of education more widely available. The success of this system of instruction was the introduction of a second age class, that of the *paides*, or boys, at the Olympic games in 632 (Pausanias 5.8.9); and boys were allowed to compete from the inception of the Pythian games in 586 or 582 (Pausanias 10.7.5). The Greeks called boys from the ages of about seven to fourteen years of age *paides*, but it seems that those allowed to officially compete and exercise in the gymnasion were roughly in their early teens. While we do not know the precise age requirements for these events, the youngest recorded victor is Damsicus of Messene, age twelve, who won the boys' *stadion* race in 368 at Olympia.

Perhaps as early as the sixth century, the crown games (the games that conferred wreaths to the victors) of Isthmia and Nemea included a third age category, that of the beardless youths, or *ageneioi*. Another term for this age group is *neaniskos* (*neaniskoi*), probably males in their middle to late teens. While boys were not admitted to long-distance or armed races or to the heavy combat events (*pankration*), it seems they did compete in most other events. There were boys' running and pentathlon events in the Pythian games at Delphi, and the programs at Isthmia and Nemea were the same for boys and men.

The extent to which athletic competitions and their awards were deeply embedded in Greek culture is evidenced by the fact that Athenians announced the birth of a boy by placing an olive wreath on their door—a wish for his future glory as a victor in the games. Sources speak admiringly of ambitious mothers who pushed their sons into training for the games. Pausanias (6.1.5), in describing the honorific statues at Olympia, credits the mother of the boy runner Deinolochos of Elis for getting her son involved in the games; apparently she was motivated by a vision that she had while pregnant of holding her baby boy crowned with a wreath. Both children's toys and their parent's poignant memorials to those who had departed too young suggest an obsession with athletics at all levels. Although females were barred from competing in the games and from instruction in the gymnasia, a curious object testifies to the fact that the fascination with athletics was not gender specific. A terracotta ball, possibly a rattle from sixth-century Athens, now in the Museum of Fine Arts, Boston (13.169), is painted in black-figure technique with scenes of javelin and discus throwers. It is surprisingly inscribed "I belong to Myrrine, yeah!" So palaistra scenes might be deemed appropriate for a girl's toy.

Athletic training and competition were clearly a family affair. There are many cases of multiple victors within several generations of one family. As Philostratos notes, "The Olympic victor who comes from a family of Olympic victors is more glorious."[3] According to the law of Elis it was forbidden for married women to attend the games. One mother, Pherenike (or Kallipateira), risked the penalty of death and disguised herself as her son's trainer in order to accompany him to Olympia. At the announcement of his victory, she was discovered but was spared being thrown from the cliffs on the road to Olympia because she was the daughter of the famous boxer Diagoras of Rhodes. He had three sons who were boxers and pancratiasts and two grandsons who were boxers.[4] This anecdote reveals several important facts, including the fame of certain families of victors and the tradition that an adult family member would escort the boys for the long journey and training period in Elis and the competition during the Olympic festival, usually about six weeks. The rich were able to hire private trainers for their sons who supervised their daily routines at the local gymnasia and traveled with them as coaches to the games. Perhaps it was this same privileged clientele who created a market for the many black- and red-figured vases depicting shorter nude boys standing opposite draped bearded men with the training sticks or receiving honorific leafy branches and woolen ribbons from them.[5] In the context of the Greek symposion and gymnasion, young Greek men engaged in physical and mental exercises under the supervision of their elders and superiors. The ideal of love between older and younger men seems to have functioned as a means for young aristocratic men to make the transition into society, sexual maturity, and eventually marriage.

Although fewer exact statistics can be ascertained from ancient texts and inscriptions about boy champions than about men, there is no doubt that the Greeks honored the boy victors, to judge by the poems and sculptural monuments created to their glory. Pausanias lists many inscriptions and describes statues dedicated to boy victors, especially boxers and wrestlers, in his sixth book on Eleia. A relatively recent archaeological find from the island of

Kos of an inscription honoring a boy wrestler who defeated four others at Olympia in the late first century B.C. confirms the widespread tradition of honoring young victors.[6]

Most images of young athletes survive in the depictions of Athenian vase painters. These artists used a few simple conventions to indicate youth, namely by making the nude boys shorter, less muscular, and hairless. This practice is best observed on a series of prize amphora for the victors of the boys' competitions in the Panathenaic games at Athens. These officially-produced jars held about forty liters of precious olive oil from the sacred groves of Athens measured out by the Treasurers of the Acropolis. The quantity of vessels awarded varied according to the event and the age of the competitors. For example, fifty amphorae valued at about $45,000 were given to the winner of the *stadion* in the boy's class, while sixty went to the winner in the youth's (teens) class. A boy in the pentathlon received thirty jars, or about $27,000.[7] Scenes of the events for which the athlete was awarded the prize are painted on one side of these large amphorae. Boys are shown in boxing and wrestling matches flanked by bearded draped trainers who prod them with forked sticks in order to correct their positions and point out their fouls.[8]

Young boys played a significant role in equestrian events as well. Given the small size of Greek horses, lightweight jockeys were sought to ride the horses of the aristocratic owners who were the official entrants and victors of these competitions. Probably one of the most animated and lively depictions of a boy athlete is that of the lifesize bronze of a jockey riding on the horse in full gallop found in the sea off the island of Euboea (Cape Artemision); it is now in the National Museum of Athens.[9] The small young jockey with Ethiopian features rode bareback and without stirrups; he could well have been a highly trained boy slave of the horse's owner.

Pausanias makes clear that women did not compete in the crown games and that married women were not allowed to attend the games, at least at Olympia. There was, however, a tradition of competitive footraces for girls, *parthenoi*. At Olympia, girls entered the races for three different age groups as part of the festival of Hera organized by sixteen of the most respected women of Elis. Pausanias (5.16.4) describes how the participants looked during these races: "Their hair hangs down, a chiton reaches to a little above the knee, and the right shoulder is bared as far as the breast." [10] The victors were allowed the honors of statues and paintings like those of their male counterparts. [11] The length of the footrace for the virgins was only five-sixths of the course of the Olympic stadium, but the female winners were also crowned with olive wreaths. [12]

Works of art are our best evidence for Greek athletics, but representations of female athletes are rare. When we take into account the serendipity of finds, the hundreds of male athletes painted on vases—providing details about actual events, training, hygiene, and victory—are impressive and reveal the level to which sixth- and fifth-century Greek society was passionate about competitive sports. It must have been quite extensive, as Aristotle in the fourth century still felt the need to urge moderation in training the young. In presenting his treatise on the proper education of children he wrote, "Those who train their children in athletics to the exclusion of other necessities make their children truly vulgar." He also warns that overly vigorous training before puberty stunts growth. [13] Aristotle's concerns alert us to a society mad about the games and athletics—today's "soccer moms" would have been at home in ancient Greece.

1. For a recent discussion of the meaning of the kouroi within the context of Greek society, see Gloria Ferrari, *Figures of Speech: Men and Maidens in Ancient Greece* (Chicago, 2002), esp. 112–26.

2. For a study of ancient Greek education, see H. I. Marrou, *A History of Education in Antiquity* (Madison, 1982), esp. 36–45.

3. Philostratos, *Lives of the Sophists*, 611, trans. Wilmer C. Wright, Loeb Classical Library (Cambridge, 1968), 277.

4. Pausanias 6.7; anecdote is also told in Judith Swaddling, *The Ancient Olympic Games* (Austin, 1999), p. 41. On Diagoras, the *periodonikes* or all-circuit victor for boxing, see Mark Golden, *Sport and Society in Ancient Greece* (Cambridge, 1998), 108.

5. The importance of trainers for the young is made clear by the many references to them in the odes of Pindar for the boy victors; see ibid., 83.

6. Ibid., 105

7. See ibid., 142. For a table listing the different quantities of awards, see Martin Bentz, *Panathenaïsche Preisamphoren* (Basel, 1998), 14.

8. See examples in ibid. of boy wrestlers from Harvard University Art Museum and Baltimore Museum of Art, nos. 5.175 and 5.177, pl. 80; standing youths of different heights with their trainers from Naples, no. 5.090, pl. 69; wrestlers from the National Museum, Athens, no. 5.198, pl. 87; and boxers from the British Museum, London, nos. 4.014 and 4.015, pl. 106.

9. Sean Hemmingway, *The Horse and Jockey from Artemision: A Bronze Equestrian Monument of the Hellenistic Period* (Berkeley, forthcoming).

10. Stephen G. Miller, *Arete: Greek Sports from Ancient Sources* (Berkeley and Los Angeles, 1991), 102.

11. For other festivals (Isthmia, Sikyon, Epidauros, and Sparta in the Peloponnesos; Delphi, Brauron, and Munichion in central Greece), see Anne Reese and Irini Vallera-Richerson, *Athletries: The Untold History of Ancient Greek Women Athletes* (Costa Mesa, 2002), 76, 143, 147, 155, 158; and Thomas Scanlon, *Eros and Greek Athletics* (Oxford, 2002), 102–5, 371, n. 25.

12. For a recent discussion of the games for girls as part of their passage into womanhood, see Matthew Dillon, *Girls and Women in Classical Greek Religion* (London and New York, 2002), 131–32, 211–13. On the Spartan females, see Thomas F. Scanlon, "Virgineum Gymnasium: Spartan Females and Early Greek Athletics," *Archaeology of the Olympics*, ed. Wendy J. Raschke (Madison, 1988), 185–215.

13. Aristotle, *Politics* 1338–1339a, translation from Miller, *Arete*, 150.

If you yourself, sitting in the midst of the spectators,
were to see manly perfection, physical beauty, wonderful condition,
mighty skill, irresistible strength, daring rivalry, indomitable resolution,
and inexpressible ardor for victory. . . .
I am sure that you would never have stopped praising and cheering
and clapping . . . that is the training we give our young men,
expecting them to become stout guardians of our city,
and that we shall live in freedom through them.

—Lucian, *Anacharsis or Athletics* 12, 30

STRIVING FOR EXCELLENCE: ANCIENT GREEK CHILDHOOD AND THE OLYMPIC SPIRIT

Jenifer Neils

Eight works of art from the Boston Museum of Fine Arts and one loan from the Hood Museum of Dartmouth College have been added to the exhibition to illustrate the role of athletics in the life of the ancient Greek youth. Although they do not represent every aspect of Greek sport and competition, these objects provide a sampling of the athletic and equestrian activities that figured in the major religious festivals held since 776 B.C. in Greece. Of these the most famous in antiquity, as now, was the festival of Zeus held at Olympia, known to us as the Olympics.[1] Although the events of the modern games, first held in Athens in 1896, are not the same, the spirit of the Olympics lives on in its modern revival. Athleticism, then as now, is a value cherished worldwide and nurtured among the youth of all countries.

In the four years leading up to our Olympiads, rigorous training is required of all contenders. In antiquity, a month before the Olympics commenced, prospective competitors were required to reside and train in the town of Elis, supervised by the officials of the games. Three objects discussed here (cats. B, C, D) are vases depicting young athletes exercising in the palaistra under the guidance of their trainers. What will strike modern viewers immediately is that the ancient Greeks trained and competed in the nude. An inscription found at Megara states that an Olympic competitor named Orsippos decided he could run faster without a loincloth and so discarded it during the fifteenth Olympiad (720 B.C.) and ever since athletes competed without clothes. The Greek word *gymnasion* indicates a place where athletes strip to exercise in the nude (*gymnos*). These gymnasiums and palaistras can be recognized in vase paintings because the artists frequently show the athletes' hygiene kits hanging on the wall in the vicinity of the nude athletes and their cloaked trainers.

Once they secured a victory in the games, athletes often dedicated a statue of themselves or a piece of athletic equipment in thanks to the gods. A bronze statuette of a diskobolos (cat. E) and an inscribed marble discus (cat. F)—both of which may have been dedications—illustrate that quintessential Greek sport, the discus throw. Some festivals, like that held every four years in Athens known as the Panathenaia, awarded the equivalent of cash prices to first-, second-, and third-place winners. Three capacious Panathenaic-shaped amphoras (cats. G, H, I), once filled with valuable olive oil, represent the prizes awarded at this premier Athenian festival for which nearly two thousand such vases were commissioned every four years. The most aristocratic events in ancient times were the equestrian contests, because then, as now, only the wealthy could afford to own and maintain race horses. A small chalcedony gem (cat. J) illustrates the most prestigious of these equestrian events, the chariot race.

The Olympics were an enduring spectacle; they lasted more than a millennium, from 776 B.C. to A.D. 395, and were responsible for many important monuments of ancient Greek art. Through Pierre de Coubertin's vision we can once again enjoy this dramatic display of athleticism, and the modern Olympics continue to inspire works of art today, some of which are even influenced by ancient art. A case in point are the mascots of the 2004 Olympic games: Athena and Phevos, two children, sister and brother. Their forms are based on that of an early Greek doll-like figurine from Tegea in the Athens National Archaeological Museum. A similar but somewhat later doll, also known as a bell-shaped idol, is the charming example in Boston (cat. A) on loan to this exhibition. The choice of a doll-like shape and of children as mascots conveys the idea of pleasure in games that derives from our childhood. The simplicity and joy, vitality and creativity of children's games are also imbued in the spirit of the modern Olympics. With this spirit in our hearts and minds, let the games begin.

1. For further information on the ancient Olympics, see Yalouris 1979; Raschke 1988; Tzachou-Alexandri 1989; Lippolis 1992; Vanhove 1992; Swaddling 1999; La Regina 2003. For the Panathenaia, see Neils 1992; Neils-Tracy 2003.

A. BELL-SHAPED DOLL OR IDOL

Boeotian terracotta, Late Geometric, ca. 720–700 B.C.

H. 30 cm; without legs 23.5 cm

Ex coll.: Edward Perry Warren

Museum of Fine Arts, Boston

Henry Lillie Pierce Fund, 1898 (98.891)

A typical product of late-eighth-century Boeotia is the terracotta doll or idol. The voluminous bell-like bodies of these figurines were shaped on the potter's wheel, with the head, neck, and arms handmade. They are often identified as dolls because the legs are formed separately and attached to the hollow inside of the body by means of leather, metal, or string, so that they can move like the limbs of later Greek dolls. Characteristically these figurines have extremely long necks, little heads with prominent jug ears, small modeled breasts, and a variety of painted decoration. The style of the decoration relates closely to that found on a group of Late Geometric *oinochoai* (wine jugs) from Boeotia and so confirms an early date for these objects of about 720–700 B.C.

The Boston doll-idol is decorated with typical Boeotian ornament. Most distinctive is the eight-arm swastika that appears in the exact center of her body. Below it is a double-axe motif flanked by water birds with drooping tails. Above the breasts are triple concentric circles and between them hangs a fringed pendantlike object. Swastikas, a common Geometric motif, appear on the figurine's arms as well as in the interstices of the double axe. Special attention has been paid to the face: the brows and rims of the eyes are painted with white beads inserted as the irises; the mouth is an incised slit and the ears are pierced; the hair is painted in long wavy lines, two in front of each ear and twelve down the back of the neck. As on many of these doll figurines, the top of the head is pierced for hanging. Somewhat enigmatic is the long painted fringe hanging below the figurine's arms and extending around to the back; it may be an attempt to depict the "girdle fashioned with a hundred tassels" donned by Hera in the fourteenth book of the *Iliad* (14.181) when she is about to seduce Zeus. (Such string skirts continue to be worn to this day by unmarried peasant women to signal their availability as wives and potential mothers.) On her feet the figurine wears sandals indicated in paint. The fact that the legs are a slightly different color clay suggests that they may have belonged to another doll or idol.

Although none of the half-dozen extant Boeotian figurines comes from a specific context, other similar bell-shaped figures with dangling legs have been found in children's graves, suggesting that they may have functioned as playthings in ancient times. Whatever the original purpose of the Boston doll-idol, she is a charming specimen of Greek Geometric art.

Published: K. M. Elderkin, "Jointed Dolls in Antiquity," *American Journal of Archaeology* 34 (1930): 459–60, fig. 6; J. Dörig, "Von griechischen Puppen," *Antike Kunst* 1 (1958): 50, no. 5; Vermeule 1963, 34, no. 28; R. A. Higgins, *Greek Terracottas* (London, 1967), xx, 23, pl. 9E; F. R. Grace, *Archaic Sculpture in Boeotia* (Rome, 1969), 10–15, fig. 2; A. Ruckert, *Frühe Keramik Böotiens*, Antike Kunst Beiheft 10 (Bern, 1976), 38–39, 112–13, no. Te2, pl. 29.2; J. Boardman, *Early Greek Vase Painting* (London, 1998), 64, fig. 101; V. Jeammet, *Idoles-Cloches de Béotie* (Paris, 2003), 17, fig. 17.

On dolls in general, see COA 267–68. On the string skirt, see E. J. W. Barber, *Prehistoric Textiles* (Princeton, 1991), 255–58; E. J. W. Barber, *Women's Work: The First 20,000 Years* (New York, 1994), 54–66. The winged *potnia theron* on the well-known Boeotioan Late Geometric amphora in Athens (National Museum, 220) is also wearing long tassels. For a ninth-century infant burial (Ialysos grave 141) with a bell-shaped terracotta figure, see J. N. Coldstream, *Geometric Greece* (New York, 1977). 46. He argues (p. 202) that the Boeotian figurines are dolls.

B. ATHLETES TRAINING IN THE PALAISTRA
Attic red-figure *psykter* (wine cooler), attributed to Phintias, ca. 520–515 B.C.
H. 34.4 cm; Diam. 26.9 cm
From Italy
Ex colls.: Alfred Bourguignon; Edward Perry Warren
Museum of Fine Arts, Boston
Henry Lillie Pierce Fund, 1901 (1901.8019)

Before a Greek athlete competed in the Olympics or any of the other religious festivals with athletic contests, he had to learn and practice his sport in the palaistra under the watchful eye of a trainer (*paidotribes*). Many painted vases produced in ancient Athens illustrate this important phase of athletics. With its eight nude athletes and four cloaked trainers, this vase presents one of the fullest pictures of the training activities that took place daily in sixth-century Athens. Three pairs of athletes are involved with their javelins; the fourth pair is wrestling. In the case of the wrestlers, it is clear that they are not competing because the upright youth offers no resistance and is, in fact, letting himself be thrown by his partner, who grasps him around the waist. The trainer at the left is providing instructions: note his extended right index finger, indicating a speaking gesture. A second trainer at the right, also bearded, cloaked, wearing a wreath, and holding the trainer's long stick, is a silent observer.

The *acontists*, or javelin-throwers, are also not competing but are receiving instruction, probably in the proper preparation of the javelin. Unlike the modern metal javelin, the ancient Greek prototype was made of wood and equipped with a metal ferrule, or point, to enable it to stick in the ground. Its propulsion was aided by the loop of a leather strap wrapped around the shaft at the point of balance (known as the *ankyle*) into which the *acontist* inserted one or two fingers. On the opposite side of the vase from the wrestlers, two youths are testing the leather straps, rendered as red loops, of their javelins braced on the ground, as is the far figure in the next group to the left. Since his right foot is clearly off the ground, he seems to be caught in the moment of planting his javelin. The other figure in this twosome resembles an athlete since he is nude, but he is acting like a trainer with his right hand raised in a speaking gesture. The third pair of *acontists*, just to the left of the wrestlers, is under the supervision of a more youthful (i.e., unbearded) trainer. While one athlete bends over to pick up two javelins, his partner holds his javelin breast high, the fingers of his right hand are inserted in the strap, and with his left he is pressing the javelin forward to tighten the loop. Reading this uninterrupted narrative from left to right, the viewer can see three stages of javelin preparation (planting the javelin in the ground, adjusting the strap, and tightening the loop) followed by wrestling.

In the ancient games throwing the javelin was not an independent event but was part of the pentathlon that consisted of running, discus throw, jumping, javelin, and wrestling. Although it is not known how the pentathlon was scored, one could win without wrestling, so that presumably was the last event. It seems that the javelin throw came just before wrestling, and thus it makes sense that this vase painter associated these two activities. The choice also allowed him to show off his ability to depict bodies in a variety of complex poses as well as his competence in the newly discovered art of foreshortening.

A conspicuous feature of this vase and of many contemporary ones painted by the group of early red-figure vase-painters known as the Pioneers is the use of painted inscriptions. Alongside each figure, usually starting at his head, is a line of thick red letters giving his name (often with letters missing or incorrect). The *paidotribeis* are Simon, Ptoiodoros, Hegias, and Epilykos. The wrestlers are Eudemos and Sos(t)ratos, while the *acontists* are named Xenophon, Phayllos, Philon, Etearchos, So(s)tratos, and E(u)krates. Of these the name Phayllos is the most famous, for he was an athlete from the Greek colony of Kroton in southern Italy who won three times at the Pythian games at Delphi—twice in the pentathlon and once in wrestling. He went on to command the only ship provided by the western Greeks at the battle of Salamis (480–479 B.C.) and to have a statue of himself erected on the Athenian Akropolis. If he was born circa 545 B.C., he was probably about twenty-five or thirty when this vase was painted, and so the figure labeled "Phayllos" just might be a "portrait" of him (as may be four images of Phayllos on other Pioneer vases). He is depicted as a nude, beardless athlete, holding a javelin point up and speaking to Xenophon. Unlike the other athletes who wear simple fillets in their hair, he wears a wreath like the trainers.

The *psykter* is unusual in the wide repertoire of
Greek vases and its mushroom-shaped body is distinctive.
It functioned as a wine cooler and was set afloat in a
krater (mixing bowl) filled with cold water or snow. For
this reason its decoration was restricted to the upper half.
As a specialty item for the symposium, it was a luxury
vessel that went out of fashion about sixty years after this
vase was made. Two other red-figure *psykters* produced by
contemporaries of Phintias also display an uninterrupted
sequence of athletic scenes but of greater variety. Phintias
probably pioneered the idea, and it was taken up by his
followers as a fashionable theme for the centerpiece of
the aristocratic symposium.

Published: Caskey-Beazley 1954, 3–6 no. 67; *ARV*² 24, 11, and 1620;
Yalouris 1979, 211, fig. 115; Poliakoff 1987, 44, fig. 34; *Addenda*²
155; Lippolis 1992, 97, fig. 85.

On the javelin throw, see Yalouris 1979, 196–201; Sweet 1987, 52–55.
On Phayllos, see Caskey-Beazley 1954, 4–5, who list three additional
paintings of this athlete; a fourth is in the J. Paul Getty Museum,
Malibu (84.AE.63). For the inscriptions, see H. R. Immerwahr,
Attic Script: A Survey (Oxford, 1990), 67, no. 392. On the *psykter*,
see S. Drougou, *Der attische Psykter* (Würzburg, 1975). The
two contemporary *psykters* with athletes are attributed to Oltos
(Metropolitan Museum of Art, New York, 1910.210.18; *ARV*² 54, 7)
and the Pezzino Group (Zurich University, 4039; *ARV*² 1621, 3 bis).
See C. Isler-Kerényi, "Dal ginnasio al simposio," *Quaderni ticinese*
16 (1987): 47–85.

C. *SKYPHOS* WITH JUMPERS
Attic red-figure *skyphos*, attributed to the Brygos Painter, ca. 480 B.C.
H. 14.4 cm; Diam. 17.8 cm
Found in Greece in 1901
Museum of Fine Arts, Boston
James Fund and by Special Contribution, 1910 (10.176)

One of the masterpieces of the early-fifth-century Athenian cup-painter whom we call the Brygos Painter, this deep cup, or *skyphos*, presents an ideal format for two complementary scenes from the palaistra. The setting is clearly indicated by the array of athletic equipment: a pick to loosen the ground under one handle, a discus bag hanging in the background and two crossed javelins on both sides, a cushioned stool holding one athlete's mantle, his hygiene implements (strigil, sponge, and *aryballos*, or oil flask) suspended above it, and a small slave boy holding the other athlete's walking stick, sponge, and *aryballos*. Both nude athletes are accompanied by their trainers, who wear cloaks (*himatia*) with black borders and hold knobbed walking sticks as well as the customary trainer's stick.

In spite of these similarities, the artist has varied the two scenes, most noticeably in the poses of the athletes and their *halteres*, or jumping weights. Holding a pair of stone weights, one jumper is preparing to take his position. The other, equipped with lead weights, is already in the third position of the long jump with both arms held out in front of the body. His backward inclining body and forward left leg also indicate the final upward swing of the weights at the end of the run. (For the next phase of the long jump, see cat. D). These youths are also pentathletes, for the running long jump was not a separate event but part of the pentathlon. Their muscular bodies show that they are all-round athletes, trained to perform in a number of events.

One of the most charming figures on the vase is the young, blonde slave boy near the handle. The eminent scholar Beazley called him "one of the first, one of the only, real children in vase painting." Although many realistic images of children exist later in the fifth century, this sympathetic depiction of a small child is one of the earliest. The Brygos Painter was fond of young servant boys for he painted them on a number of his symposium vases. On Attic grave stelae of the fourth century it became common to commemorate an athletic youth accompanied by his slave holding an *aryballos* or other athletic equipment. On both marble reliefs and vase paintings, this child servant acts as a status symbol for his aristocratic master.

Published: Caskey-Beazley 1931, 18–20, pl. 7; *ARV*² 381, 173; Vermeule 1963, 107, no. 88; *Paralipomena* 368; *Addenda*² 227; Lippolis 1992, 94–95, figs. 82–83.

For the running broad jump, see Yalouris 1979, 176–87; Sweet 1987, 46–51. For the Brygos Painter, see A. Cambitoglou, *The Brygos Painter* (Sydney, 1968). For the slave child on Attic stelae, see C. Clairmont, *Classical Attic Tombstones* (Kilchberg, 1993), and *COA* 307, no. 125.

D. *KYLIX* WITH PENTATHLETES

Attic red-figure *kylix*, attributed to Onesimos, ca. 500–490 B.C.
H. 9 cm; Diam. 22.5 cm
Said to be from Orvieto, Italy
Ex colls.: Alfred Bourguignon, Naples; Edward Perry Warren
Museum of Fine Arts, Boston
Henry Lillie Pierce Fund, 1901 (01.8020)

The interior and two exterior sides of this fine red-figure cup by Onesimos are devoted to two events of the pentathlon: the discus throw and the running long jump. In all three scenes we see youths practicing in the palaistra indicated either by the ubiquitous athletic kit (sponge, *aryballos*, and strigil) and pair of javelins (interior) or by a pair of jumping weights strung up on the wall and a pick lying on the ground (exterior). On each exterior side two nude athletes are working out under the watchful eye of their young, energetic trainer, who extends his long stick threateningly. One side features two jumpers with lead *halteres* in hand. One is simply moving to the left in preparation for a jump, while his companion is in dramatic mid-flight, his legs and arms extended in front of him. In the next instance he will jettison his weights behind him to extend the length of his landing. A third jumper (only partially preserved) stands on the other side of the cup with his weights extended, rather like one of the jumpers on the Brygos Painter's *skyphos* (cat. C). In front of him is a youth, leaning back slightly and with a discus lying along his right forearm. He looks as if he is about to begin the backward swing of the discus but his stance is incorrectly rendered. Perhaps that is the reason for the *paidotribes'* extended rod.

Beautifully adapted to the circular field of the interior is the curved body of another *diskobolos* farther along in his throw. He is depicted in the back view favored by this artist with clear definition of the clavicles and spine. Unlike the discus on the exterior, which is depicted in profile, this one is shown in three-quarter view. The faint bit of peach fuzz on the boy's cheek, rendered with dilute glaze, indicates that this handsome boy is an adolescent on the brink of manhood. He is wreathed as are the other athletes on this cup.

Published: Caskey-Beazley 1954, 29–31, pl. 40; ARV² 321, 22; *Paralipomena* 359; Yalouris 1979, 185 fig. 88; Sweet 1987, 48, pl. 13; *Addenda²* 215; Lippolis 1992, 24–25, figs. 13–14.

For the discus throw, see Yalouris 1979, 188–95; Sweet 1987, 40–45.

E. *DISKOBOLOS*
Bronze statuette, Early Classical, ca. 480 B.C.
H. 14.9 cm
From Greece
Ex coll.: Edward Perry Warren
Museum of Fine Arts, Boston
Gift by Contribution, 1901 (01.7480)

With his left arm raised overhead, his lowered right arm holding the discus, and his forward right leg, this bronze *diskobolos* resembles his painted contemporary on the cup by Onesimos (D above). However, his pose is stiffer and some of his features, like eyes and hand, are disproportionately large. Nonetheless, the vigorous modeling of his torso, his muscular legs, and his broad chest show that the sculptor recognized the characteristics of a pentathlete. The medium of bronze allowed him to produce a figure in motion with widely splayed limbs that capture the action of the discus throw.

Bronze statuettes such as this one were frequently dedicated at sanctuaries like Olympia, presumably by victorious athletes, either in thanks for a victory achieved or in hopes of one. In antiquity the most famous statue of a *diskobolos* was that cast by Myron in bronze that now exists only in marble Roman copies. The famous mid-fifth-century sculptor Polykleitos is also credited with a statue of an athlete holding a discus.

Published: Vermeule 1963, 115, no. 95; M. B. Comstock and C. C. Vermeule, *Greek, Etruscan and Roman Bronzes: The Museum of Fine Arts Boston* (Boston, 1971), 42, no. 42; Vanhove 1992, 206 no. 161.

For athletic statuettes, see R. Thomas, *Athletenstatuetten der Spätarchaik und des strengen Stils* (Rome 1981).

F. INSCRIBED DISCUS
Attic marble, Archaic period, ca. 500 B.C.
Diam. 28.5 cm; Wt. (as preserved) 6.7 kg (14 lb. 10 oz.)
Ex colls.: Edward Perry Warren; Albert Gallatin; Catherine Gallatin
Museum of Fine Arts, Boston
Gift in Memory of Albert Gallatin, 1987 (1987.621)

Although the modern discus is a standard size (22 cm in diameter) and weight (2 kg), the extant ancient examples vary considerably. They are made of bronze, lead, and marble and range from 16 to 34 cm in diameter and from 1.25 to 9 kg in weight, with the average being 2.5 kg. Some of these, like this heavy marble example from the late sixth century b.c., were votive offerings and not intended for use in the games. According to Pausanias (6.19.4) at ancient Olympia three official discuses for use in the pentathlon were stored in the treasury of the Sicyonians.

This marble discus was both painted and inscribed. A round black tondo can still be seen in the center and it once was decorated with a red horseman riding to the right with a lance, perhaps an emblem of the man who owned the discus. The roughly incised inscription *EK TON E[PI]ON*, part of which is missing, means literally "from the burial mound" but can be interpreted as "from the games held at the burial mound." The most famous example of funeral games held for a dead warrior are those Achilles conducted at Troy in honor of his slain comrade Patroklos, but the practice continued into historical times. The inscriptions on this discus and another probably found with it (Metropolitan Museum of Art, 1985.11.4) indicate that these marble discuses were prizes awarded at funeral games.

Published: Sotheby's, sale cat., May 27, 1929, no. 89; P. Jacobstahl, *Diskoi* (Berlin and Leipzig, 1933), 14–18, fig. 8; C. C. Vermeule and M. Comstock, *Sculpture in Stone and Bronze in the Museum of Fine Arts, Boston: Additions to the Collections of Greek, Etruscan and Roman Art, 1971–1988* (Boston, 1989), 20, no. 6.

For funeral games, see L. E. Roller, "Funeral Games for Historical Persons," *Stadion* 7 (1981): 1–18.

G. PANATHENAIC PRIZE AMPHORA WITH LONG-DISTANCE RUNNERS

Attic black-figure amphora, attributed to the Euphiletos Painter, ca. 530–520 B.C.
H. 60.7 cm; Diam. 40.4 cm
From Vulci, Italy
Ex colls.: Prince Torlonia; Edward Perry Warren
Museum of Fine Arts, Boston
Henry Lillie Pierce Fund, 1899 (1899.520)

For the first half century of the ancient Olympics, the short footrace for men was the one and only contest. Known as the *stadion*, it was a sprint from one end of the stadium to the other, or six hundred Greek feet, which at Olympia is approximately two hundred meters. Given the popularity of this event and to allow for more contestants, additional footraces were soon incorporated into the games. In 724 B.C. the *diaulos* (twice as long as the *stadion*) was added, and in 720 B.C. the *dolichos*, a long-distance race, was included as well, but according to our ancient sources its length varied at different sites, anywhere from seven to twenty-four *stades*, or one to three miles. There were twenty lanes at Olympia and in order to qualify for one, runners had to compete in and win a trial heat. An intermediate race of four *stades*, or eight hundred meters, known as the *hippios* was introduced at the Panathenaic games held in Athens since 566 B.C. as well at other sites.

It is fairly easy to determine which race runners are competing in by the position of their arms. Like joggers, the five men on this vase bend their elbows and hold their arms close to their bodies. Their legs are splayed wide in the position common to most depictions of runners, but they are leaning forward into the race unlike the longest distance runners, who are upright. Therefore, one could conclude that they are competing in the *hippios*. Their pronounced muscular thighs and chests demonstrate the conditioning necessary for this demanding event. The ages of the runners vary as indicated by their beards or lack thereof.

The other side of this vase is painted with the canonical decoration of all Panathenaic prize amphoras, namely those filled with oil and awarded as prizes at the games held every four years in honor of Athena in Athens. The goddess Athena, armed with spear and shield, strides to the left framed by two Doric columns atop which cocks are poised. The official inscription *TON ATHENETHEN ATHLON* ("one of the prizes at Athens") runs vertically along the left-hand column. What distinguishes these otherwise prescribed Athenas by various Athenian painters are her dress and shield device. The so-called Euphiletos Painter, who decorated prize amphoras in the last quarter of the sixth century B.C., depicts Athena in elaborately incised drapery with radiating folds. The shield device is often an animal; on the Boston example the protome of a panther in added white contrasts with the black background.

Published: *ABV* 322, 7; *Addenda*² 87; *CVA* Boston 1 (USA 14) pl. 55; Bentz 1998, 128, pls. 16–17, no. 6.058.

On the *hippios*, see Yalouris 1979, 168 and 174, fig. 79. On the Panathenaia, see Neils 1992.

H. PANATHENAIC PRIZE AMPHORA WITH WRESTLERS

Attic black-figure amphora, attributed to the Berlin Painter, ca. 480–470 B.C.

H. 62.2 cm; Diam. 40.6 cm

Ex coll.: Mr. and Mrs. Ray Winfield Smith

Hood Museum of Art, Dartmouth College, Hanover, New Hampshire

Gift of Mr. and Mrs. Ray Winfield Smith, Class of 1918 (C.959.53)

Wrestling, or *pale* as it was known in Greek, was the first contest added to the Olympic program (in 708 B.C.) that was not a footrace. It was both part of the pentathlon and an independent event. Wrestling began from a standing position, and from here wrestlers would try to throw their opponents to the ground. The object of this contest was to win three falls, with a fall meaning that the opponent's back, shoulders, or hips touched the ground. Competitors were sorted into pairs by drawing lots, and some famous wrestlers like Milo of Kroton could achieve a "dustless" (*akoniti*) win when no one dared compete against them.

This prize amphora by the accomplished red-figure painter known as the Berlin Painter bears a unique scene of two bearded wrestlers and a judge with forked stick at the left. It is unusual because the wrestlers are neither in the head-on starting position nor in a wrestling hold, but rather one is chasing and attempting to trip the other. He has grabbed his opponent by the left shoulder and right elbow and has wrenched his upper body into a frontal position. The incised lines on the victim's left arm suggest that his arm is being twisted, so one might think the more violent *pankration* is being depicted. In the next moment the disadvantaged wrestler will no doubt be tripped by the right foot of his opponent which is raised to the level of his knee. Tripping was allowed in both wrestling and the *pankration*.

The other side of this prize amphora shows the requisite striding Athena between Doric columns topped by cocks. What distinguishes the Berlin Painter's Panathenaics is the *gorgoneion* used as the shield device of Athena. If one compares the bodies of the Berlin Painter's wrestlers with the boxers on the next Panathenaic amphora (cat. I), one can tell that the later artist painted in the newer red-figure technique and was adept at showing figures in complex poses. The workshop of this painter produced some twenty Panathenaic prize vases, probably for more than one festival.

Published: *ARV²* 214; *Paralipomena* 177, 2 ter; Poliakoff 1987, 39, fig. 29; Neils 1992, 171, no. 39, illus. pp. 28 and 30; B. A. Sparkes, *The Red and the Black* (London and New York, 1996), 119 fig. V:4; Bentz 1998, 145, no. 5.074, pls. 64–65; Neils-Tracy 2003, 22, fig. 19.

For wrestling, see Yalouris 1979, 202–13; Poliakoff 1987, 23–53; Sweet 1987, 60–67. For the Berlin Painter's Panathenaics, see Bentz 1998, 144–46.

I. PANATHENAIC AMPHORA WITH BOXERS

Attic black-figure amphora, attributed to the Mastos Painter, ca. 530–520 B.C.
H. 60.2 cm; Diam. 42.1 cm
Ex colls.: W. H. Forman; Edward Perry Warren
Museum of Fine Arts, Boston
Henry Lillie Pierce Fund, 1901 (01.8127)

The obverse of this amphora of Panathenaic shape shows that it is not a prize vase, for it lacks the official inscription designating it as "one of the prizes from Athens." In all other respects—size, iconography, ornament—it resembles a prize vase, and the Mastos Painter, to whom it is attributed, did decorate five official vases. Perhaps he simply forgot to paint on the prize inscription or possibly there is something amiss with the reverse decoration.

On this side there is a boxing match (or *pankration?*) between a bearded man and an unbearded youth. They are flanked by a nude youth at the left waiting his turn to compete and by a draped judge at the right holding aloft a long stick. It looks as if the bout is at an end because the youth who has fallen to the ground raises his right index finger in a gesture that signals defeat. The bearded man standing over him appears ready to deliver another blow but the judge is intervening to halt the match. Boxing was the most brutal of Greek sports because the contestants wore no protective headgear and delivered most blows to the head, resulting in facial deformities and cauliflower ears. The vase-painter has not indicated the *himantes*, or leather thongs, usually wrapped around the hands and wrists of boxers, so this painting has also been identified as depicting the *pankration*, a combination of boxing and wrestling in which no holds were barred. Only biting and gouging were prohibited. Because this seems to be a mismatch between a youth and an older man, the painting may have been deemed inappropriate for the Panathenaic festival.

Published: *ABV* 260, 28; Vermeule 1963, 81 no. 74b; *CVA* Boston 1 (USA 14) pl. 56; Yalouris 1979, 231, fig. 133; *Addenda²* 68.

For boxing, see Yalouris 1979, 216–25; Poliakoff 1987, 68–88; Sweet 1987, 68–80. For the *pankration*, see Yalouris 1979, 226–31; Poliakoff 1987, 54–63; Sweet 1987, 81–88. For the *himantes*, see *COA* 253, no. 55. For Panathenaic prize amphoras by the Mastos Painter, see Bentz 1998, 127 (Workshop of the Lysippides Painter).

J. GEM WITH CHARIOTEER

Scaraboid intaglio, chalcedony, late 5th century B.C.
L. 2.6 cm
Ex coll.: Edward Perry Warren
Museum of Fine Arts, Boston
Francis Bartlett Donation, 1923 (23.582)

This exquisite gem represents on a miniature scale the epitome of Classical art. A charioteer in a long robe is driving a *biga* pulled by two lively stallions. While the horses and driver are in profile, the four-spoked wheel is depicted in three-quarter view, indicating that the chariot is being shown in the demanding moment of the turn. The far horse is in a full gallop while the near horse is being restrained so as to make the turn around the *kampter*. One can even detect this action in the small detail of the position of the charioteer's hands, one pulling the reins, the other letting them loose. The horizontal tail and flying skirt of the charioteer serve to emphasize the dramatic forward movement of this racing chariot. Because of the stylistic similarity of this intaglio to the silver coins minted in Syracuse and signed by the artists Kimon and Euainetos, the gem can be dated circa 413–403 B.C. Since it was purchased in Athens, it may have been produced there.

Chariot racing was part of most local festivals and no doubt was one of the most popular spectator sports, just as horse-racing is today. In the Olympics of 416 B.C. the Athenian Alkibiades entered seven chariot teams and won first, second, and third places. His reasons for entering so many equestrian teams are recorded by his son:

> My father saw that the festival at Olympia was beloved and admired by all men,
> and it was there that the Greeks made a display of wealth and strength of body and training,
> and the athletes were envied while the cities of the victors became renowned.
> In addition, he believed . . . that services to that festival offered credit to the city in the eyes
> of the whole of Greece.
>
> —Isokrates, *Team of Horses* 32–33

Published: A. Furtwängler, *Antiken Gemmen* 2 (Berlin, 1900), 38, pl. 65 no. 4; C. C. Vermeule, "Chariot Groups in Fifth-Century Greek Sculpture," *Journal of Hellenic Studies* 75 (1955): 112–13, fig. 16; Vermeule 1963, 123, 135, no. 119; J. Boardman, *Greek Gems and Finger Rings*, rev. ed. (London, 2001), 292, no. 561, pl. 561. J. D. Beazley, *The Lewes House Collection of Ancient Gems*, rev. ed. (London, 2002), 112, no. 55.

For equestrian contests, see Yalouris 1979, 232–41; Sweet 1987, 89–95.

ABBREVIATIONS

ABV	Beazley, J. D. *Attic Black-figure Vase-painters*. Oxford, 1956.
Addenda²	Carpenter, T. H. *Beazley Addenda*. 2nd ed. Oxford, 1989.
ARV²	Beazley, J. D. *Attic Red-figure Vase-painters*. 2nd ed. Oxford, 1963.
COA	Neils, J., and and J. H. Oakley. *Coming of Age in Ancient Greece: Images of Childhood from the Classical Past*. New Haven, 2003.
CVA	*Corpus Vasorum Antiquorum*.
Paralipomena	Beazley, J. D. *Paralipomena*. Oxford, 1971.

BIBLIOGRAPHY

Bentz 1998
  Bentz, M. *Panathenäische Preisamphoren*. Antike Kunst Beiheft 18. Basel, 1998.
Caskey and Beazley 1931
  Caskey, L. D., and J. D. Beazley *Attic Vase Paintings in the Museum of Fine Arts, Boston*. Vol. 1. Oxford, 1931.
Caskey and Beazley 1954
  Caskey, L. D., and J. D. Beazley. *Attic Vase Paintings in the Museum of Fine Arts, Boston*. Vol. 2. Oxford, 1954.
Dierichs 2002
  Dierichs, A. *Von der Götter Geburt und der Frauen Niederkunft*. Mainz, 2002.
La Regina 2003
  La Regina, A. *Nike: Il Gioco e la Vittoria*. Rome, 2003.
Lewis 2002
  Lewis, S. *The Athenian Woman: An Iconographic Handbook*. London, 2002.
Lippolis 1992
  Lippolis, E. *Gli eroi di Olimpia*. Taranto, 1992.
Neils 1992
  Neils, J. *Goddess and Polis: The Panathenaic Festival in Ancient Athens*. Hanover and Princeton, 1992.
Neils and Tracy 2003
  Neils, J., and S. V. Tracy. *The Games at Athens*. Agora Picture Book 25. Athens, 2003.
Poliakoff 1987
  Poliakoff, M. B. *Combat Sports in the Ancient World*. New Haven, 1987.
Raschke 1988
  Raschke, W. J. *The Archaeology of the Olympics*. Madison, 1988.
Reeder 1995
  Reeder, E. D. *Pandora: Women in Classical Greece*. Princeton, 1995.
Swaddling 1999
  Swaddling, J. *The Ancient Olympic Games*. 2nd ed. London, 1999.
Sweet 1987
  Sweet, W. E. *Sport and Recreation in Ancient Greece*. New York and Oxford, 1987.
Tzachou-Alexandri 1989
  Tzachou-Alexandri, O. *Mind and Body: Athletic Contests in Ancient Greece*. Athens, 1989.
Vanhove 1992
  Vanhove, D. *Le Sport dans la Grèce antique*. Brussels, 1992.
Vermeule 1963
  Vermeule, C. C. *Greek Etruscan and Roman Art: The Classical Collections of the Museum of Fine Arts, Boston*. Boston, 1963.
Yalouris 1979
  Yalouris, N. *The Eternal Olympics*. New Rochelle, N.Y., 1979.